PHILLIP UNTHANK

GET A life

Make the most of your life with proactive personal planning

Re^think

First published in Great Britain in 2025
by Rethink Press (www.rethinkpress.com)

© Copyright Phillip Unthank

All rights reserved. No part of this publication may be reproduced, stored in or introduced into a retrieval system, or transmitted, in any form, or by any means (electronic, mechanical, photocopying, recording or otherwise) without the prior written permission of the publisher.

The right of Phillip Unthank to be identified as the author of this work has been asserted by him in accordance with the Copyright, Designs and Patents Act 1988.

This book is sold subject to the condition that it shall not, by way of trade or otherwise, be lent, resold, hired out, or otherwise circulated without the publisher's prior consent in any form of binding or cover other than that in which it is published and without a similar condition including this condition being imposed on the subsequent purchaser.

*To Laurie, for being my biggest supporter, and
always up for one more adventure…*

Contents

Introduction	**1**
1 A Journey, Not A Destination	**9**
Carving out time	10
Look up	14
Social anxiety	16
Don't wait for rainy days…	18
Commercial exploration	21
Summary	23
2 Keeping Work In Its Place	**25**
Work/sleep/repeat	27
Working opportunities	33
How badly do you want it?	38
Summary	38

3	**Connecting With Others**	**41**
	Hold onto your friends	42
	If need be, go on your own	45
	Getting to know people	46
	Summary	51
4	**A Sense Of Occasion**	**53**
	Any excuse…	54
	Making occasions special	58
	Summary	61
5	**Making The Most Of Leisure**	**63**
	Catch the day	65
	Doing things on a budget	69
	Summary	74
6	**Planning**	**77**
	Keep a list	81
	Digital or paper?	85
	Sources of information	88
	Work backwards	91
	No such thing as overpreparation	93
	Delisting	95
	Summary	96

7	**Travel**	**99**
	Timetables	101
	Booking	104
	Packing	107
	Sightseeing	109
	Capturing memories	112
	Summary	114
8	**Take Your Pick**	**117**
	A wide perspective	118
	Go with the flow	122
	Curiosity	125
	Hobbies and projects	126
	Summary	130
9	**Happiness**	**133**
	Happiness as a goal	135
	Positively charged	138
	Keep moving	142
	Summary	144

Conclusion   **147**

Appendix 1 – Two-Day Tour Of New York   **151**
    Itinerary for day one   151
    Itinerary for day two   154

Appendix 2 – Checklists   **157**
    Travelling abroad   157
    Travelling with children   158
    Camping and hiking   159

Resources   **161**
    Printed materials   161
    Digital   162
    Planners   163

Acknowledgements   **165**

The Author   **167**

Introduction

About five years ago I had a strange water cooler moment. It was a typical Monday morning and I was in the kitchen at the office getting my first cup of tea when a colleague of mine, Joseph, walked in. I asked him how his weekend had been.

'Fine,' he said.

'What did you get up to?' I asked. I was just trying to be polite and show an interest. He was a nice young man and soon to be a father.

'We didn't do anything; we just cleaned and watched TV.'

'Oh, OK,' I said, and went to leave.

Joseph stopped me and asked what I'd got up to. 'Well,' I said 'we went up to Huntington Beach and saw the civil war reenactment. It's the largest one on the West Coast – four hundred volunteers! My son loved it. The next day we hit the Huntington Garden. It has one of the finest art collections in the world – beautiful grounds, too.' I smiled and again went to leave. Then it happened. Joseph started yelling, 'You always do that! You always do something amazing; you're always doing that!'

He was angry with me? I couldn't understand it. What had I possibly done to offend him? We went to my office to explore this hostility further and I got to understand that he was resentful. He and his wife never did anything; they just stayed home and watched TV every weekend while, in his mind, I was out living a wild and eventful life.

I told Joseph the truth: 'I too used to be just like you. I never did anything interesting, I never had stories to tell and the most exciting thing that happened was a new movie coming out. However, I discovered the secret to a more interesting life.'

I then shared with Joseph my method of personal proactive planning – and he loved it. He followed all the steps you'll find in the following pages and it gave him more stories, more things to plan for and more things to look forward to. He bought a planner and started telling other people about the plans he was making.

INTRODUCTION

That's when I knew I had the ingredients of a potent method that could help other people. Over the years I've shared this knowledge with friends and colleagues, and now I've written it down in the hopes of reaching even more people.

Looking back, I find it hard to believe that I had been just like him ten years before, simply existing from one work week to the next. I felt like everyone was having fun but me. I wasn't popular or beautiful. I always felt like an outsider. I didn't seem to get the invitation to life, however many times I checked the mailbox. I had no hobbies of note. I didn't come from a well-connected family. I was plain and ordinary in every way.

But eventually a story that my dad used to tell came to mind, and that's when the penny dropped. This was a saying burned into my heart and soul by my father: 'Anyone can be cold, wet and miserable. It takes no effort at all.' He joined the army back in the 1950s as a boy soldier – at just fifteen years old. The British Army had just stumbled out of World War ll and was ramping up for World War III with the Soviet Bloc. That meant the Allies had to get some practice in ahead of the big push. These play battles were called 'exercises', and entailed large-scale combat manoeuvres that took place all over the German countryside.

My father noticed when he was deployed that the supply chain often failed – well, it was the British Army after all. Food trucks failed to turn up, tents leaked, no one was given a map and units got lost or cut off on a regular basis.

He found that if he thought ahead and brought his own blanket along in case the higher-ups forgot to provide them, then he stayed warm. If he brought some extra rations then he remained fed, even if the meal tent didn't show. Those who didn't think ahead this way ended up cold, hungry and miserable.

Reflecting on this lesson, I realised that it was no good me sitting around waiting for something to happen: I needed to do something about it. If I wanted to have excitement, if I wanted to forge memories worth having and moments to be proud of, I would have to make them happen myself. No one was going to organise them for me. If you take just one thing away from this book, make it this piece of wisdom.

If you're thinking that you're too busy to do any of this, working all hours, keeping up with the demands of running a household etc, may I draw your attention to Parkinson's principle: 'Work expands to fill the time available.'[1] If you don't carve out time to spend with your family or to do different projects, work will fill the void. There's always something else to do at work, and yet you can still look back and get the sense that you've achieved nothing. Therefore it was that I woke

---

[1] CN Northcote, 'Parkinson's Law', *The Economist* (19 November 1955), www.economist.com/news/1955/11/19/parkinsons-law, accessed January 2025

INTRODUCTION

up in my early twenties and felt like I wasn't achieving anything. 'Stuff' tends to fill the space and stops you from ticking off anything from that vague list of 'things you'd like to do' that you carry in your head.

What I want is for you to have the same rewards that I've had from using my methodology; for you to look back on the last quarter or the last year and say, 'We *did* do this; we *did* do that. That's a great memory. We had the most fantastic time there.' Without actively planning ahead, you'll just let the molasses of life trickle through your fingers. You'll just go back to the same routine; you'll watch TV, go to bed early and you won't achieve anything.

By 'achieve', I don't mean promotion, status, wealth or luxury items. These can turn out to be the most disappointing 'achievements' of all. I remember an entrepreneur I worked with telling me he was going to get a new car – a Lamborghini Huracan, no less. The joy didn't last long. After the short-lived excitement of turning heads had faded, he found he hated the incessant roar of the engine and the fact that everyone felt entitled to come up and talk to him about it or take photos. This car had cost him $320 grand and he looked a million dollars in it, but after six months he was sick of all the razzmatazz that came with it. What a hollow achievement.

Even a coveted promotion can leave you feeling flat once the thrill of the chase is over, and the extent of the weight on your shoulders becomes clear. Yet at the same time, you may find yourself eyeing up the next promotion, so it seems as if we are never satisfied, always chasing after new goals. It's great to have the salary increase, and maybe a corner office, but these things always come at a price. I'm not saying you shouldn't be ambitious, or that you shouldn't work hard, especially if you have responsibility for others and commitments. You just need to keep a sense of perspective.

As far as my own career is concerned, I think it was not so much ambition as my unacknowledged desire for a richer life that saw me try lots of different jobs before settling on what became my career. My first real move after a few starter jobs was to become a bank manager, then I went into sales support, and finally into accounting and finance. Although in the end it was not for me, my stint as a bank manager gave me a valuable basis for both my professional and personal life. All human life walks into your office and tells you about their hopes, dreams and fears. The range of aspirations and anxieties I came across was staggering – you couldn't hope for a better source of insight into what makes people tick.

My advice isn't just aimed at people with busy jobs. Sure, it's important to set boundaries at work, but the homemaker and the carer need boundaries too. My mother used to clean the bathroom every day – was that really necessary? The daily round of cook, wash, eat, sleep, repeat needs to be disrupted from time to time with memorable activities and events.

I also want to make clear that you don't need a lot of money to do this. I remember having a great time with my family not so long ago, when we decided to try out an experiment for kids: create a container out of balloons that you could put an egg into, throw it out of a second storey window and have the egg land intact. We just bought a load of balloons and tried that one Sunday. My son and I each thought we were the winner, but in truth my wife won, with her design like a Coach handbag complete with handle. I've got a video of her creation coming down, and again, when I showed the guys at work, someone said, 'Man, you always do the most fun things with your family.'

This book is not about showing you how to be a better person. I don't want to tell you how to live your life. It's simply to give you some tips, techniques and suggestions for how to enrich your life, based on my extensive trial and error.

If anything good came out of the Covid-19 pandemic, it's that it showed us that many things we thought were important were in fact not. It showed us that when we had the space to notice them, it was small things that mattered. Once we could no longer go out and have a cup of tea with a friend, we realised how much we'd taken small treats like these for granted. Little wins, it turns out, can mean a lot.

My aim with this book is that you should always have something to look forward to, whether it's the simple pleasure of reconnecting with an old pal, or having a major adventure that could take some pretty intensive research and planning. I'll be making the case for taking steps to enrich your life in this way, providing some ideas and inspirations for getting you started, and giving you the organisational tools to take control (the 'Resources' section at the back of the book contains practical templates and links).

John Lennon is supposed to have said, 'Life is what happens when you are busy making other plans.'[2] Well, I would argue that life is what happens and passes you by if you don't make plans to participate in and enjoy it.

---

[2] Although this quote is often attributed to John Lennon, it actually comes from US journalist and cartoonist Allen Saunders, and appeared in the *Reader's Digest* in 1957.

ONE
A Journey, Not A Destination

When I was a kid, we were introduced to lots of careers. One in particular caught my imagination, and that was the job of bank manager. We were shown case studies of managers working with commerce to build and plan whole neighbourhoods, to help people buy homes and to finance factories and industry. It was instrumental to society; I wanted to do that. No one I knew wanted to do that… Everyone else wanted to be a firefighter or a farmer (it was rural Hampshire, after all).

A friend referred me to a trainee manager role on offer at a local bank. I'd told a lot of people that I wanted to be a bank manager; the opportunity came my way and so I went for it. I applied, was hired and started straight away. I flourished at the bank and before long was managing my own branch.

But I realised that though I had, in the words of the satnav, 'reached my destination', I didn't want to stay there. What I really enjoyed were the challenges, the variety and the learning that came with the journey towards what I was aiming for.

Carving out time

Work has always been important to me. I'm not one of those people who thinks you should abandon the mundane things in life to 'follow your dreams'. I have, probably like you do, responsibilities to people other than myself. Therefore, work has to come first sometimes. However, if you let work be the be-all and end-all of your life, you will be missing out on so much that could enrich it.

I firmly believe that, in life, we only have room for three large blocks. For me currently these are: work, family and friends. However, at times these blocks have been work, family and study, or relationship, work and work. It is possible to have four blocks, but only temporarily; when you have too much, you start dropping things.

For one friend of mine the three things were: work, extended family and his football club. He was an avid fan and never missed a game – weekends, midweek, somewhere in Europe – you name it. He followed the chat forums constantly; it was a huge part of his life and left little time for anything else.

If you let them, these three blocks will fill your days. Unless you are disciplined, you will never carve out time for adventure or novelty. This is why you must keep things in perspective and apply some of that highly efficient work planning energy to personal planning, too.

The power list

It turns out that the real power list is not a collection of names of the rich and famous, but your humble to-do list. I love a list. Needless to say, I have a work to-do list: a daily list annotated according to priority, with the top three items having their own numbered boxes. However, I also have a personal weekly to-do list to help me plan time with my family and friends, and for the leisure projects I'm working on.

When it comes to creating effective lists, there is a great deal to be said for the Ivy Lee method. Back in 1918, Ivy Lee was much in demand as a productivity consultant.[3] He had a simple methodology for achieving maximum productivity:

---

3   J Clear, 'The Ivy Lee Method: The daily routine experts recommend for peak productivity' (JamesClear.com, no date), https://jamesclear.com/ivy-lee, accessed January 2025

1. Keep a list of the six most important tasks to do each day – and don't have more than six.

2. Prioritise the six items.

3. Tackle the first task first, and complete it before moving on to the second one.

4. Keep moving through the tasks. Carry over any tasks you haven't finished to the next day.

5. Repeat steps 1–4 every day.

I'll be going into a lot more detail about the art and science of planning, but the thing to remember here is that freeing up blocks of time that you intend to fill with the things that delight you most is the first step towards enriching your life. It's where you temporarily step off the treadmill that we are all subject to (unless you're insanely rich, don't need to work and have a full complement of personal staff to tend to your everyday needs).

Once you've carved out a block of time and filled it with something that you really want to do for yourself, you've broken the mould – of the necessary routine, of the same old same old, of an unvarying round of work, sleep, repeat. The beauty of the work list is that it helps free up leisure time, and this record of your planning stands as evidence of what you have done; the power of your personal list is that you are more likely to actually do things you've written down.

An example of my personal list for 2024 is below:

Quarter 1 2024			Quarter 2 2024		
January	February	March	April	May	June
Book special restaurant for wife's birthday	Plan day in LA ahead of business evening do	Buy new hiking boots	Easter parade	Hiking Iron Mtn	Picnic at Balboa-Park
Book Lego Convention in OC	Book Global Entry interview for March	Book Shakespeare Utah Festival and play tickets	Send out invites for picnic	UK trip	CTP exam
Book February flight to Denver to see Dave and plan itinerary	Research and book Cincinnati ahead of next month's Ark Encounter trip	Book UK trip and share itinerary with friends, confirm timings	Order Jake's passport renewal	CFO conference in Washington	Wellness day at hospital
Book theatre dates in quarter	Book full day wellness check for June	Confirm additional days in Vegas with wife and plan itinerary	Partial solar eclipse – order glasses	LV work trip and add two days with wife	Get bikes serviced for Bike the Bay ride
	Book Keane tickets for September	Book nuclear reactor tour well in advance of August for security clearance	Wii U down from garage to play Jake	Plan trips in Q3 and confirm with friends including blacksmithing, jetski trip, fishing trip and half marathon	Book Bike the Bay
			Book theatre dates in quarter	Book birthday weekend Big Bear cabin for August	August tickets
			Book half marathon tickets and friends	Confirm when Gwendal here in Q3	Book snorkelling tour for July for me and Jake
			Book study time off for June exam		Book chef lesson date night for birthday August

Phillip's planner

I love to look back on my plans and recall the interesting places I saw, the friends and family I connected with – even the madcap activities that ended up frightening the life out of me.

Look up

As soon as you look up and beyond your usual horizons, there's no telling what you might see, as the story of the discovery of the Altamira cave paintings demonstrates.

CASE STUDY: It takes a child...

The Cave of Altamira, in northern Spain, is renowned for its prehistoric paintings, the earliest examples of which were painted 36,000 years ago, during the Upper Paleolithic Period. The cave itself was discovered in 1868 by Modesto Cubillas, but it was studied in detail by Marcelina Sanz de Sautuola.[4] He started exploring the caves in 1875 but it was not until 1879, in what we can only assume was an early form of 'take-your-daughter-to-work' day, that his daughter drew his attention to the pictures of bison adorning the ceiling of the caves. They had been there all along, but he had literally had his head down, examining the ground, while she was simply letting her gaze wander...

---

4   A Kiely, 'The 7 most important prehistoric cave paintings in the world' (thecollector.com, 11 November 2022), www.thecollector.com/most-important-cave-paintings-in-the-world, accessed January 2025

A JOURNEY, NOT A DESTINATION

Anyone's life can be a bit of a slog at times, but there's no reason why you shouldn't appreciate the flowers along the wayside as you negotiate the journey. Excitement and adventure shouldn't be confined to holidays.

It helps to have – or to cultivate – a sense of curiosity. Even as a child, I enjoyed exploring new worlds through old movies and books – lots and lots of books: I practically lived at the library. I thought my small-town library, which only occupied the same area as my modest home, was amazing. It contained stories about all kinds of life outside of my world. I read every type of book I could lay my hands on, from biographies of the great and good, to science fiction; from philosophy to arts and crafts. I just loved seeing it all and hearing the voices of other people – and often discovering that other people had had the same strange thoughts and opinions that I had.

By cultivating a genuine sense of wonder about the world around you and a desire to understand how all of it works, you'll begin to see all kinds of doors start to open – limitless opportunities for exploration and enrichment. If you have the means, why not hire all the Sherpas you need and attempt to climb Everest? At the other extreme, you'll find there are hundreds of opportunities closer to home that don't require millions of dollars to make the most of them. There is so much out there to discover, entirely scalable to match your circumstances. You just need to keep your eyes open to it.

CASE STUDY: Waterworks

My dad had a massive stroke at the age of fifty-three. From being a very active man – a career soldier – he became paralysed down the right side of his body. However, he was still always researching and enquiring. He once wrote to the local water authority asking how they stored and cleaned the water. They wrote back with a ton of leaflets and a personalised letter inviting him up for a special tour of their water treatment plant. He took them up on their offer, and enjoyed the visit hugely. (And the water authority staff were delighted to find someone so interested in their work!)

Adventure is right there at your fingertips; all it takes is an inquiring mind and application.

Social anxiety

What often keeps us confined within the humdrum daily round is worry about what other people think of us: that we're too frivolous, extravagant, pretentious, etc. Small children are blissfully untroubled by such worries (which causes its own problems, but that's for another book). Given half a chance they will follow their own interests to an obsessive degree, but in adulthood we tend to leave all this behind and follow the course expected of us.

I, perhaps like you, certainly worry about what other people think of me. I mentally kick myself when I say or do the wrong thing, fretting that other people will misinterpret my motives and meanings. However, it's all unnecessary. What I've learned over the years is that people we don't know don't worry about us at all. Being concerned that, say, dressing in a particular outfit will cause strangers – who you will never get to know – to disapprove of or laugh at you is bordering on the ridiculous. I'm not suggesting you wear your dressing gown to work, rather that you put such social pressures into perspective. Worry about social status is a big cause of depression and misery, yet it shouldn't be.

TOP TIP

Nine times out of ten, the people whose opinions you are so worried about aren't thinking about you at all. They have their own problems front and centre in their minds, and don't even notice you.

Similarly, never let popular opinion about what is or isn't a cool activity or interest inhibit your choices. Whether your 'thing' is high-brow or low-brow, trendy or nerdy, go for it – bear in mind that it takes a lot more mental agility to play bingo successfully than it does to drift around an art gallery wallowing in the images.

Have you ever heard the phrase, 'Comparison is the thief of joy'? Maybe you think you haven't got time to stop and smell the roses because that's not the way to get on in life, and you want to have what your colleague at the next desk has, or your neighbour. This is what happens when you compare 'up'. I remember when I was working in sales support, there was a sales manager who earned five times my salary but was totally miserable in his job. You never know what is going on behind closed doors, and your assumptions are more than likely false. I'm not necessarily saying be content with your lot – you can always strive to do better, whether it leads to promotions and more money or not – rather, I'm saying don't dwell on the 'successes' of others.

Don't wait for rainy days…

Your capacity to enjoy your journey through life will be limited if you make the opportunities you go after too contingent on other things, whether that's money, promotions or just the stars being in alignment. This applies whether it's some trivial treat or a major project.

> **CASE STUDY: The $5 stumbling block**
>
> I saw a book I really wanted on offer at half price, but I didn't buy it because I was between paydays. I waited a year for that offer to be repeated, but it never was. What was I thinking? The variance was marginal, just $5, but I was content to postpone my purchase almost indefinitely. At the same time, I was perfectly happy to pay over the odds for a sandwich at the airport or at a service station, but the $5 for a book I desperately wanted seemed a bridge too far. Ridiculous.

The above type of 'lizard brain' thinking, where our instinctive, survival-driven impulses override rational decision-making, is going on all the time. Do your best to be aware of it and act rationally instead – though this is often easier said than done.

Postponing your happiness or fulfilment for a 'someday' moment is futile and unnecessary. I'm not suggesting you spend all your money today. (I save aggressively myself when I want to.) I'm just saying be realistic about what you are holding out for and why. Is the saving you're chasing a material one? If you 'overspent' today and then the price dropped, what would that actually mean to you? Once you commit to a purchase, stop checking on subsequent prices – whatever happens, it's not going to make you happy.

Studies have found that the first price you attach to a thing or activity is an 'anchor' of its value after that.[5] You are constantly looking to get a bargain or pay below that cost for it. The value of this item becomes what you deem it to be. The only question that matters, though, is: is this item what I want and can I afford it? The cost is relatively artificial.

There can also be a big difference between the cost of an item and its value to you, which can mean that the most expensive item is not necessarily the one that is best for you. Sometimes cheaper is more valuable – my experience of getting a law degree demonstrates this well.

CASE STUDY: How much for a legal eagle?

I was always envious of people in the law profession. So many of the greats from history were lawyers: Jefferson, Samuel Adams, Disraeli, Lenin (not keen on his politics, but he could argue well!). Who were these people? What was the magic spell conferred by their legal training? What were these sacred texts that ruled our lives? I was fascinated by all this and wanted to obtain a law degree.

This is a tall order when you're an adult with a full-time job and personal commitments – to my family and to

---

5   Y Zong and X Guo, 'An experimental study on anchoring effect of consumers' price judgment based on consumers' experiencing scenes', *Frontiers in Psychology*, 13 (2022), www.frontiersin.org/journals/psychology/articles/10.3389/fpsyg.2022.794135/full, accessed February 2025

the mortgage company! At first, the project appeared impossible, but I looked to the UK and found a cheap law course meant for lawyers in training, complete with onsite training every quarter. I could not attend those 'essential' events, but my independent study and dedication meant that I overcame the odds and after four years finished with a 2:1 – an achievement that far surpassed the results of my first degree, despite the vastly different learning conditions.

Commercial exploration

'Commercial exploration' is a technique used by companies to test the water and estimate how successful a proposed new product or service is going to be. In the personal realm, I also see it as a valuable way to find out what sorts of activities and events will provide you with the excitement and enrichment you're seeking.

It's often hard to tell what will take off and what will fade into obscurity. Who could have predicted that Twitter's (now X) capability to host snappy 140-character posts in real time would prove such a runaway success? This is why, especially when you're starting out on carving out leisure time and planning how to make good use of it, you should keep an open mind.

CASE STUDY: Cake fun

A while back, I discovered one of the most unexpectedly satisfying activities when I baked a cake for the Cubs with my son. The challenge was for it to be a genuine father and son project. We made a huge pyramid of multicoloured cake layers (and a lot of mess) – and won the prize! It wasn't the most artistic cake, but it was the most exuberant and the one that was most obviously a collaboration.

I took it into work the next day and my colleagues loved it. People came up to me and thanked me, and two people even asked for the recipe. I loved all the genuine praise and kind feedback. I commented to a colleague on how awesome the experience had been and she replied, 'Yeah, why do you think I bring in cake so often?'

Positive feedback and a sense of connection are just two of the types of reward you can gain from branching out and prioritising the personal. Bear in mind, too, that what you want from your down time may vary according to what point you're at in your journey, be it a professional one or a domestic one. For example, if your daily routine entails being a domestic deity, you might hanker after the kind of activity that entails wearing clothes that are guaranteed not to be used as handkerchiefs and not having to worry about where you put your glass down.

I'll be exploring how to identify what exactly you want to do further in Chapter Eight, so that you can consider this in the context of travel and planning.

Summary

One way or another, most of us spend a lot of time fulfilling our duties and it's easy to forget that you're allowed to – and should! – enjoy yourself along the way. Make sure you don't miss out on enjoyment by:

- Keeping a list of the activities and events you'd like to take part in
- Earmarking blocks of time that you could use for leisure and spending with family and friends
- Developing your curiosity about the world around you and a sense of exploration
- Seizing opportunities as they arise, rather than waiting for some mythical perfect time
- Being open-minded about the types of activity you could enjoy

So how do you build adventure and novelty into your everyday routine, whether that involves turning up at the office or keeping domestic chaos at bay? Read on to find out.

TWO
Keeping Work In Its Place

At a time when I was feeling particularly bogged down at work, I had a life-changing conversation with a friend about my dissatisfaction (though a year later he couldn't even remember that we'd had it). The truth of my father's saying about it taking no effort at all to be miserable had dawned on me, but I wasn't sure how to go about fixing things. My friend suggested that I should write down five things that I wanted to do over the course of the next year. I thought that was a great idea, and drew up a quick list.

I judged it was better to come up with a list spontaneously, and not waste more time agonising over it. I thought of all the things I'd always wanted to do but hadn't yet achieved. I was reasonable about it, though – no 'go to the moon' or anything like that. This is the list I came up with:

- **Sailing:** I'd spent a lot of time on research boats when I did my ocean science degree, mostly below decks staring at instruments, but didn't you need to be rich and successful to do 'proper' sailing?

- **Gliding:** It looked fun, and it was cheaper than flying planes. Putting it on my list spurred me to find out more about it.

- **Do an accounting course and get a new job:** I had realised that there were people out there putting far fewer hours into their working week and earning more than me. Doing a night course would give me a feel for whether this area was right for me. As soon as I started thinking about a new job, I began noticing opportunities.

- **Learn an instrument:** The most common regret in the celebrity interviews at the back of the *Daily Mail* was never learning an instrument. I didn't want to risk having that same regret, so I decided to take up the guitar.

- **A 'grand day out':** Some things are best done with friends, so I decided to plan a memorable excursion with a friend. The day would involve test driving cars that couldn't be more different from my little rust bucket, some fast food and the aforementioned gliding.

Even just compiling the list was fun. It gave me topics to research, something to look forward to, a reason to recruit friends to share some of the events with and then memories to look back on with them. Once I'd actually had some adventures I knew this was a habit I wanted to maintain.

Work/sleep/repeat

Life is exhausting: work asks a lot from us during the day and it can take time to decompress in the evenings and at weekends. It's easy to concentrate on surviving the day, coming home from work, perhaps grabbing a glass of wine and just relaxing. Family time and home commitments are real and can expand to take up any slack we have.

If you don't break out of your autopilot routine from time to time, you'll eventually come to and feel as if you've achieved nothing. This feeling of drifting is a rotten one that I want to save you from. Instead, I want you to have adventures great and small and share them with the ones you love.

Routine

The problem with routines is that they can get too comfortable and give you excuses not to do things. However, they are not completely without value. The best routines make it possible to undertake a lot of activities fairly efficiently, and I would argue that it's better to have too much than too little to do. There's a lot of truth in the saying, 'The Devil makes work for idle hands' and it turns out that a lot of the idle rich are not very happy – no doubt because not having to work to survive can end up making you lazy.

To guard against idleness during the Covid-19 pandemic, I adopted a habit tracker to ensure that I kept up with a routine that would guarantee my mental and physical health in the face of essentially house arrest.

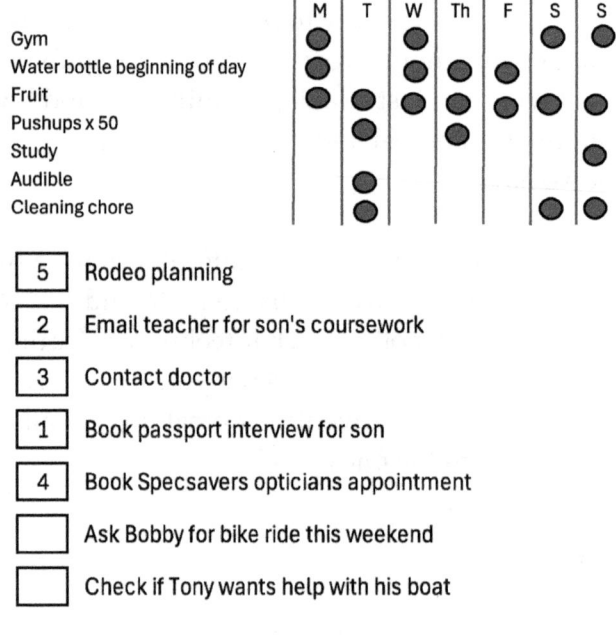

Habit tracker combined with the week's top five personal tasks

This worked so well for me that I've continued it ever since. It's an ideal way of combining the routine tasks and activities that underpin my functioning, taking care of the little one-off tasks that are also key to self-maintenance and managing family life, and keeping my eyes on the prize of big adventures.

While they are not essential, there are plenty of useful habit tracker tools available on the internet. I find it helpful to have this one at the top of my to-do list to keep myself honest about things like how many times I've been to the gym or how much water I've drunk.

Parkinson's Law

The naval historian C Northcote Parkinson formulated the law that bears his name in an essay in *The Economist* in 1955.[6] From his extensive experience of working in the British Civil Service, he had noticed that 'work expands to fill the time available'. Never mind the Civil Service – I've seen this law at work in my own family. My mother likes to go shopping in Salisbury, which is an hour and a half away by a bus that takes you through every little village along the way. When I asked her why she didn't take the train, especially as she lives near the station, she replied, 'Well, I've got nothing else to do…'

Unless you're disciplined, you can easily fill up slack time with things like randomly checking your email, watching Instagram reels (I'm guilty of this

---

6   CN Northcote, 'Parkinson's Law', *The Economist* (19 November 1955), www.economist.com/news/1955/11/19/parkinsons-law, accessed January 2025

one – I can't resist a golden retriever video!), making another cup of tea, etc. However, it is exactly this time that you can use to work on your projects, plan your next adventure or keep up with your friends. The cumulative impact on your life of using this time more intentionally will be tremendous.

Burnout

By contrast, those who suffer from burnout tend not to observe Parkinson's Law. They try to cram as much as possible into their day, extending its hours almost indefinitely to try and accommodate everything they feel they need to achieve.

CASE STUDY: Crashing and burning

There are few more glamorous international figures than Arianna Huffington, co-founder of the *Huffington Post*. However, it's not very glamorous to wake up in a pool of your own blood, yet this is exactly what happened to her when she was working eighteen hours a day to build the *Huffington Post* website. While checking her emails one evening she fainted from sleep deprivation and exhaustion, and broke her cheekbone. It was a wake-up call for her, setting her on a course to encourage others to adopt a healthier and more balanced way of life.[7]

---

[7] S Morgan-Beckett, 'Arianna Huffington: Her wake-up call and mine' (The Huffington Post, 13 May 2014), www.huffpost.com/entry/arianna-huffington-her-wake-up-call-and-my-own_b_5291306, accessed January 2025

My advice from the last chapter, to 'look up', is also valid in this context. It's all too easy to get sucked into manic workaholism without noticing the danger you are in. Having significant events unrelated to work in your diary to look forward to helps you keep a sense of perspective and an awareness that there is a life beyond work.

Just make sure you don't go overboard with these activities instead (as someone with a bit of an addictive personality might be in danger of doing). If you overload your calendar with activity after activity every weekend, after five or six weeks of such frenzied busyness you will be drained again, but for different reasons. Over the years, I have found the sweet spot to be two weekends a month with adventure activities outside of the regular family routines, such as sports matches for your children, etc. More than that and I find I can burn out on adventure. Figure out where your sweet spot is.

Making time work for you

What's the best way to get through all the things that you need to do, and not let work or domestic duties crowd out your leisure time? This is where all those predictable concepts like 'moderation in all things', being sensible and so on come into play, but it can be difficult to see how to apply them to your daily routine.

I'm a big fan of the Pomodoro method, devised by Francesco Cirillo in the 1980s.[8] The beauty of it is that not only does it set boundaries around your 'working' time, it ensures that while you are focusing on the task in hand, you're doing so efficiently, with maximum concentration. The method is based on the knowledge that we all find it difficult to concentrate on things for much longer than 20 minutes at a time. It works like this:

1. Choose the task you want to achieve.

2. Set a kitchen timer (the method is named after the tomato-shaped one Cirillo used as a student) or the alarm on your phone, for 25 minutes.

3. Work on your task until the timer or alarm goes off.

4. Have a short break (five to ten minutes), then reset the timer and go back to your task.

5. After four 25-minute stints take a longer break, say, 20–30 minutes.

Using this technique is a good way of ensuring that you don't waste time daydreaming or on the displacement activities (eg doomscrolling on Facebook) that are so tempting when you're bored or feel blocked. If you know you have a legitimate break coming up

---

8   F Cirillo, 'The Pomodoro Technique' (FrancesCocirillo.com, no date), www.francescocirillo.com/products/the-pomodoro-technique-book/, accessed January 2025

shortly, you're far more likely to stick with focused thought and activity.

The quality of your work during these timed sessions will be so much better than when working on tasks with an open-ended approach, and you will complete them more quickly.

Another concept that you may be familiar with is Stephen Covey's 'big rocks' and 'little rocks', a useful technique for setting priorities. Covey illustrates this by asking you to imagine that you have to fill a jar with big rocks, pebbles and sand. If you fill the jar with sand (internet wormholes, cups of tea), you won't be able to fit in any of the rocks (important projects). The best method is to put the rocks in first, fit pebbles (routine admin tasks, emails, small errands) in the gaps between them and only then fill up any remaining space with sand.[9] This approach is great for helping you to decide on your priorities and keep a sense of perspective on secondary tasks. As I'll show later, it's also great for helping you to plan your leisure time.

Working opportunities

Sometimes you can build a degree of refreshing variety into your work. Again, the trick is to be alive to

---

9   SR Covey, *The Seven Habits of Highly Effective People* (Simon & Schuster, 2020)

the possibilities for doing this, which can range from simple activities that will contribute to your personal growth and your knowledge of how your company functions, to opportunities for international travel.

I'm always curious – you could even say nosy – about other people's work, so I have made it my mission, when there are quieter times in my team, to go and sit with other teams to see what they do. I've sat with the PR team, learning how they fit into the overall marketing picture. I've discovered how the IT development team creates middleware solutions; their contribution to the smooth running of the business largely goes unnoticed and unsung.

As part of getting to know other teams, I often look for an interesting lunch spot for our gatherings. Southern Indian restaurants are not that widespread in the US, so an informal outing to one makes for a memorable occasion that breaks down barriers and strengthens connections. Meeting colleagues with curiosity in this way deepens your understanding of the context you're working within and opens you up to new opportunities and potentially new friendships.

CASE STUDY: Packing my bags

For many years I worked at a software company with offices all over the world. One of those offices was located in Israel. I had always wanted to visit the Holy Land but could never afford it, and my wife had made it clear that she would never want to go, given the security concerns. I figured that the only way I would ever get to do it was through my company, so I let the right people know that if they ever needed anyone to go to the Israel office, I was happy to help.

I doggedly sowed the seeds for this goal for about three years, and eventually the internal audit team was tasked with doing a physical inspection of the Israel office. In the wake of some recent upheaval in the country, they were reluctant to go and I was promptly asked if I would consider it – I was also an accountant, even if I wasn't actually in the audit team. I was obviously delighted to help and grabbed the opportunity with both hands.

I added three days on to the trip as vacation, moving from a lovely hotel by the sea to a tiny hostel where I was surrounded by pretentious teenagers taking a summer break from uni. Faced with the challenge of negotiating, on my own, a country whose language I didn't speak, I booked myself on organised tours and travelled all over, visiting Jerusalem and the Via Dolorosa (the Way of Sorrows), the Dead Sea, Jericho, Masada, Bethlehem and the Golan Heights. The audit team were grateful that I had gone in their place, and I am eternally grateful to have had a once-in-a-lifetime experience that I would likely otherwise have missed out on.

As the above case shows, the beauty of letting others in on your plans and your aspirations is that you never know who may be able to facilitate, or even share them. As another example, I had long had an ambition to climb the Half Dome in Yosemite National Park.

This is no easy task, as you have to enter a hypercompetitive lottery to get hiking permits, while also booking a campsite (which is equally competitive). If you are American, you then have to be prepared to commit your precious work vacation time – which can be as little as ten days a year – to the task. In some post-meeting chitchat with colleagues, one guy said he had also dreamed of climbing the Half Dome but had been defeated by the administration challenge whenever he had tried. I asked him whether he would come with me if I got the tickets. He loved the idea and began training in earnest almost immediately. This was the beginning of a great friendship and a decade of fantastic hiking experiences together.

TOP TIP

If you are in a position to, make sure that you are enabling others to have adventurous and fun experiences, too. They may not be consciously planning to widen their horizons or enrich their journey through life as you are, but that doesn't mean they won't appreciate a departure from their routine.

Brokering your getaway

The big conundrum about all this is: how do you square safeguarding your leisure time with the demands of your job? This is probably a bigger problem in the US than it is in the UK, with its longer statutory holidays, more generous parental leave and paid leave allowances.

How transparent you can be about your intention to take the time that you should be entitled to for rest and relaxation will depend on the company you work for, and I accept that there will be periods when it's simply not possible to walk away. However, there are still things you can do to mitigate this. For example, you can:

- Take some short weekend city breaks if you can't get away for a longer period
- Plan a family hike in a beauty spot for a few hours on a Sunday
- Go to a sports event or a show that you might normally reserve for a special occasion

No one ever said, 'Remember that time we watched telly together?' so keep that in the back of your mind.

If you find you are regularly having to sacrifice your personal time for work, don't suffer in silence. Make sure your managers know that you are going the extra mile on their behalf. For a start, they need to know about it if only for planning purposes. Ideally, your conscientiousness will generate goodwill and reciprocation – like when my boss asked me to cancel a long-planned trip back to England, but then arranged upgrades for the whole family when we were finally able to get away.

How badly do you want it?

If something is really important to you, you will be able to achieve it. Alongside keeping work in its place, you also need to ensure your personal aspirations are realistic and relevant when planning your time. A while back, I found I had one objective on my list that I never got round to. After five years of carrying it over from one year to the next, it was pretty clear that my heart wasn't in it, so I took it off my list. There comes a time when you have to be honest with yourself.

There is no shame in doing this: you're not in competition with yourself. On no account should you feel you're doing any of these activities to keep up with others. That is an expensive and hollow carousel to find yourself on. It never ends and your sense of satisfaction will be fleeting. This is not about one-upmanship; it's about you enjoying your life. What's more, what you want from life is bound to change as you move through it. That daredevil adventure challenge that seemed so appealing in your teens may lose its allure once family ties loom larger in your life.

Summary

It's all too easy to let work invade every aspect of our lives – I'm as guilty of this as anyone – but making time for leisure is important both for yourself and for those around you.

- Routines have value in ensuring that what needs to get done gets done, but don't forget to build in opportunities for fun.

- Burnout and inactivity both have their dangers.

- Use your work time efficiently, so you can free up as much time as possible for other things.

- Be on the lookout for opportunities to build excitement and interest into your work schedule.

- Don't feel you have to do everything on your leisure list – it's OK for your priorities to change.

Family and friends form an important part of making the most of your leisure time, so in the next chapter we'll be exploring how to strengthen these bonds and widen your circle of connections.

THREE
Connecting With Others

I used to find it hard to keep up with all my friends in the UK – from college and from various jobs – because they were dotted all over the country. Social media may have given us a virtual portal to each other and allowed us all to watch people's lives unfolding, but it's just not the same as being together in person.

We sometimes travelled to see one another, but it was a pain: long distances, no direct train lines, heavy traffic. However, after some back and forth, we determined that London was easy enough for all of us to get to, and so settled on the great city as our new home and base. After all, as the saying goes, 'When a man is tired of London, he is tired of life.'

In London everything is to hand: the best restaurants, all the obvious attractions like the British Museum and the National Gallery. However, it only takes a little bit of planning and a few emails to get into some more exciting lesser-known attractions, like Prime Minister's Question Time at the Houses of Parliament, or Benjamin Franklin's house, where you can tour the tiny rooms and see actors playing the parts of those who lived there.

But the best thing about these visits is that I share them with my friends. They probably wouldn't do these things if I didn't organise them, but as it is we have fantastic experiences together, and memories to reminisce about in years to come. These unique events bring us closer in a way that just another drink at a bar or meal in a restaurant wouldn't.

Hold onto your friends

As life progresses, it somehow becomes harder to keep up with seeing friends in person. Your job takes up more of your time, you acquire family responsibilities – you know how it is. When we're young, we seem to have friends in abundance. When we're at school and college, they're practically on tap. However, as we get older, we tend to get more reserved, more standoffish, less likely to initiate a new friendship or issue an invitation. This is why it makes sense to at the very least try to hang onto the friends you already have!

If you value your friends, it's down to you to keep the contact going – no one else is going to do it for you. You have to accept that it may not always be possible to maintain contact with everyone: people's lives go through different phases, and you may find they are focusing on work or family to the exclusion of everything else. However, if these relationships fizzle out because of inaction on your part – well, you've only yourself to blame.

> **TOP TIP**
>
> Don't feel despondent over a knockback or a 'left on read' from a friend. People are busy – it doesn't mean they don't care; they're just absorbed in their own problems (and perhaps rightly so) in that moment.

My advice is to keep the door open. In the first instance text that old friend you haven't spoken to for a year or more and invite them for a happy hour catch up. Shared experiences with these friends often provide the inspiration for you to reach out with a message to them when you remember these occasions and the enjoyment you got from them.

Partners in fun

You can have fun on your own (and more on that later), but things are so much better when they're shared. Many friendships are forged through shared hardship: during army training, a torrid time at the office or facing the challenges of being a student. It's clear that shared experiences, whether wonderful or terrible, bring you together in a way that the daily routine does not.

But this is where the phrase 'horses for courses' bears remembering. Not everyone is up for everything. I wasn't able to interest any of my friends in going to see the small and esoteric clock museum in the Guildhall, so ended up going on my own. You will know which of your friends is always up for a long hike or some daredevil physical activity, and which would prefer an afternoon at an art gallery followed by an evening at the theatre.

But on the flip side, if any of your friends invites you along for an activity, I'd say go with an open mind. You never know what you might turn out to enjoy, or who you might meet.

CASE STUDY: Adventures in Wonderland

My wife saw an advertisement on Facebook for an Alice in Wonderland themed treasure hunt that was to take place in Carlsbad, California, of a weekend. It occurred to me that getting dressed up for it would make the event that bit sillier and more memorable, so that's what we did. I went as the Mad Hatter, Laurie went as Alice and our son went as the White Rabbit. We had a fantastic time wandering along the main street of Carlsbad completing theme-based challenges, with the added excitement of being treated like celebrities: as we had got dressed up, everybody wanted their photos taken with us. Great family fun!

If need be, go on your own

Although I always recommend sharing experiences with friends, I would never let the lack of someone to do an activity with, stop me from doing it – see the clock museum example above. Given my interest in doing a law degree I was keen to see a magistrates' court in action, but for some reason I couldn't interest any of my friends in this rather niche excursion. Never mind. I looked up the nearest courts and visited them all, the family court and the High Court too. It was a real eye opener and not an experience I would have wanted to miss out on.

The other possibility is that whoever you have arranged to go with will not be able to make it at the last minute. Why not press ahead anyway? You'll still see what you wanted to see, and you will probably interact with others more when you're on your own. You'll learn their stories and have a different but no less worthy experience by going alone.

CASE STUDY: Shipmates

When my wife was expecting she bought me a birthday present that she clearly wouldn't be taking part in alongside me in her condition: a four-day trip on a 'tall ship'. I would be part of the crew, along with thirty other people. I was younger then, and was one of only two people to pass the fitness test for climbing the rigging.

I can tell you, the trip was no picnic. The ship was taking on water, we had four-hours-on/four-hours-off shifts, and nothing but merciless sea all round us. It could have been hell, except that my good friend-to-be Paul and his brother were also on board and 'adopted' me. Paul and I were even charged at by the same buffalo on Catalina Island, and if that's not a bonding experience, I don't know what is. This happened twenty years ago and we are still friends today.

Getting to know people

Any solo excursion (in fact, almost any scenario: in the workplace, at the school gates, etc) can be enriched by getting to know the other people who you meet in the course of it, be they fellow punters or those in charge of the premises or the activity. Studies have actually found that talking to strangers, in particular, has mood benefits.[10]

It helps if you have a genuine interest in people, which is something that is hard to fake. However, asking

---

10 AG Walton, 'Talk to a stranger: It'll make you happier', *Chicago Booth Review* (2 December 2014), www.chicagobooth.edu/review/talk-to-a-stranger-itll-make-you-happier, accessed January 2025

someone why they are at the same event as you, or what they do, will get you a long way. Just listen and you will learn a lot. As Dale Carnegie explains in his book *How to Win Friends and Influence People*: 'People who listen are the best conversationalists.'[11]

Remember, people's favourite topic of conversation is themselves, so ask them questions and look for connections. Even if someone is not forthcoming with their personal information, questions about their favourite book or movie usually get people talking.

CASE STUDY: Offroad

I once casually asked one of my IT colleagues about his weekend and he told me about the offroad hikes he takes his family on. It turned out he had a souped-up Jeep Wrangler with all the add-ons. I was astounded! My brother had worked for Jeep when I was a kid and had given me a green model with a golden eagle on its bonnet. Ever since then I'd always wanted to drive one. The following week, my colleague brought his Jeep in and took me out for a spin, giving me a turn behind the wheel – which just goes to show how a chance conversation can lead to an unexpected connection and special experience.

---

11   D Carnegie, *How to Win Friends and Influence People* (Simon & Schuster, 2010)

Just offer

One practical way to make connections is to be alert to opportunities to help. In a work context, this could look like offering to take on a share of someone's workload if you can see that they are struggling. I've seen people break down at their desks and their colleagues simply letting tasks go undone and projects fail, with all the implications that has for others down the line.

Offering help is possibly easier to do in the workplace than elsewhere, but your neighbours, friends and family may also be in need of a hand at times. It infuriates me when people do not offer to help others when it's clear that they are drowning. We are all in this together and should be supporting one another when we can see that it is needed.

Just ask

The other side of the coin is this: if you need help, just ask for it. Some people are reluctant to ask due to a fear of refusal or rejection. Others are too stubborn, or have no interest in other people. There are others who lack faith, usually due to past experiences, that someone else might be able to support them in the way that they need.

When it comes to fear of rejection, look at it as an exercise in growing your rhino hide. If you remember what we discussed previously, nobody is thinking about you after the end of the conversation. They're focused on themselves. Therefore, it's a no-harm no-foul situation if you ask for help unsuccessfully. Let's consider the flip side. Not asking deprives you of the assistance you need. What's more, you will miss out on opportunities to make new connections, along with the ability to learn something new and broaden your horizons.

CASE STUDY: A request with consequences

On a flight from England to San Diego, I realised I had forgotten my reading glasses and wasn't going to be able to make out my passport number to fill in my landing card. I asked the woman I was sitting next to if she would read it out, and we got talking. It turned out she was a musician, and we ended up in a long conversation about learning to play – my son was learning piano at the time. Though she was not classically trained, she had released three albums and had some great insights into the differences between classical and pop music. I followed her on Instagram, and when I saw that she was coming to San Diego, we booked to go and see her at the Casbah nightclub, a small live venue. It was a terrific evening, and the gig T-shirt is still one of my son's favourites...

The consequence of not asking is usually that you stew in your own juice. I remember as a junior building society clerk being sent to a desk with a monitor that was far too low for me. After just a few hours of work at this desk on a Saturday morning, my 6'3" frame was in complete agony. The customers were great, but my neck had begun to spasm in protest at the odd angle I'd been holding it, and my shoulders and lower back weren't too happy with me either. I thought nothing of calling the facilities manager for help. It turned out he had a whole cupboard full of monitor stands, and he brought one round a short time later. After he'd finished setting me up, the desk's actual owner emerged from the meeting room. She'd been holed up in there for hours. She spotted me at her monitor, with its newly elevated position and gasped. 'How did you fix this? I've been working at that desk for years in agony.' 'Oh, really?' I said, genuinely surprised. 'I just called someone in facilities and they came right away.' 'Oh,' she huffed, taken aback. 'I never thought of that.' It turned out facilities wasn't the problem at all; she had just never asked.

Where are they coming from?

To be able to genuinely connect with people, you have to be able to see their point of view, even if it's very different from your own. We're back to the importance of listening. The fourth of Stephen Covey's *Seven Habits of Highly Effective People* is 'Think win-win.'[12] If you want to get to the position where everyone wins, the

---

12 S Covey, *The Seven Habits of Highly Effective People*

only way to reach that compromise is to get everyone's point of view. Even if the solution doesn't reflect much of what someone wanted, they still feel involved in the process rather than ignored, oppressed or victimised. This approach works whether it's applied to serious structural change in the workplace, or to organising a day out for a disparate group of friends. Also bear in mind that people sometimes rewrite history. Several months later, they may have a completely different point of view, and have almost no memory of ever having their previous perspective. This means you need to keep checking in with them when you're doing any long-term activity planning.

Summary

A sense of connection is incredibly powerful. It's particularly good for your mental health, and for keeping your brain stimulated and active. Take action now to maintain and create your connections with others:

- Make an effort to keep in touch with friends – catching up with them can be energising.
- Don't be afraid to go on activities solo; you never know who you might meet.
- Talk to people and, above all, listen to them. You will learn things, maybe build relationships and enrich their experience as well as your own.

- If you see someone struggling with something, offer to help.
- By the same token, don't hold back from asking for help yourself when you need it – we are not islands.

FOUR
A Sense Of Occasion

You might not know it, but St Patrick's Day can be truly magical. When my son was six, we told him you had to beware of leprechauns on St Patrick's Day – if one got into the house, there was no knowing what they might get up to, so we had to make sure we locked all the doors before we went out. Later on, while my wife was getting Jake into the car, I rigged the house...

When we came back, we let him discover what had been going on and raise the alarm. All his favourite toys had been hidden in a cupboard, shamrocks had been scattered all over the place – and there was green wee in the toilet! Jake raced off to see if the leprechaun had visited the other toilets. It was a delight to witness his excitement.

The following year, we suggested he set a cardboard leprechaun trap before he went to bed so he could capture the culprit. Overnight we sprinkled a trail of glitter from the windowsill leading to the cardboard trap (which we sprung, to make it look as if the leprechaun had just escaped getting caught, and chocolate coins that he had dropped when he panicked about the trap). Oh, and there was more green wee, of course.

It was a simple idea that I'd picked up from a fellow parent, but for two years running, the whole family got a huge amount of fun out of a day that doesn't usually feature on a child's radar.

Any excuse...

Occasions great and small can be a source of joy, whether they're long anticipated or more impromptu. All you have to do is be on the lookout for opportunities.

You don't have to wait for birthdays, anniversaries and the major public or religious holidays to have fun, as the example above shows. With a bit of ingenuity, all sorts of occasions offer the chance to break out of the everyday routine and enjoy yourself. Whatever national days are relevant to your family and friends, it can be a great opportunity for getting together, dressing up, eating special food and so on (leprechaun wee or its equivalent, entirely optional).

Have a look for some international or 'world days' that might take your fancy. Did you know that 1 July is International Joke Day, or that 17 February is Random Acts of Kindness Day? Again, there's a list at the back of the book, and it offers plenty of excuses for community get-togethers, activism or just having fun.

CASE STUDY: We're all going on a badge hunt

I wanted to help my son make more connections outside of school, so he joined the Cubs and then the Scouts. He made friends with other boys and we met a lot of like-minded parents who are still part of our wider friend network. I wanted Jake to get as much out of the Scouts experience as possible so we did the hikes, and he went on all the trips and camps. I also realised that going after the various badges could provide both activities for Jake and opportunities for Mum and Dad to go along for a bit of adventure as well.

The aim of the badges is to give kids an insight into all aspects of society, from how the government works (citizenship badge) to practical skills (welding badge, for example). There are 138 badges to collect, though you only need seventeen to become an Eagle. Jake now has 100 badges and we've travelled all over the country, visiting a butterfly conservatory in Arizona, walking the Virgin River in Zion National Park, and going to a stamp collector fair in Long Beach. These trips have given Jake the chance to try new activities, hobbies and potential careers, to see what he wants out of life – and his parents have had a lot of fun along the way!

Don't overlook local events as a source of celebration. Here in San Diego we have a hugely popular Christmas event called Jungle Bells that takes place at the local zoo. Going as a family or teaming up with another family to go can become a rewarding tradition.

At an even more local level, participating in community activities by making banners, hosting a stall of some sort, maybe dressing up, gets you right into the thick of the event and makes it special.

CASE STUDY: Medieval merriment

A while back, I met up with an old work colleague, Andre, for a burger and a beer and we ended up discussing our sons' scouting activities. From this I discovered that Andre had never fired a bow and arrow, and we decided that we needed to do something about that.

I found an archery gallery midway between our houses and bought us tickets for a session. We got the idea of dressing up for the occasion, so I turned up as Robin Hood, and Andre came as the Sheriff of Nottingham – much to the surprise of the other patrons, who were mostly commuters whiling away some time to let the worst of the traffic pass.

We had a great time, firing at targets and at Lord of the Rings-style goblins made by the range. Afterwards, to continue the medieval theme, we headed three doors down to a microbrewery for a tankard of mead. As we left, I saw two people fighting with hand swords in a distant car park, which set us up for another future adventure...

As the above case shows, with just a little bit of effort, even the most casual arrangement for a 'playdate' can be turned into a memorable occasion.

There's nothing to stop you creating your own personal occasions for celebration. For example, to commemorate a particularly exciting or even silly day in your family's or your friends' lives – anything from, say, the anniversary of your child learning to ride a bike to the hundredth birthday of your house. You get the picture – any excuse for a bit of fun.

Don't miss out

While it's great to be spontaneous about things and take advantage of opportunities that appear unexpectedly, not keeping abreast of organised events means you'll only become aware of them after the fact, and then you may have to wait a year until they come round again. I'll provide more information in the planning section, but getting the dates of any recurring events into your calendar as soon as they're announced ensures that you won't miss them, that you don't plan other clashing events, and that you have plenty of time to prepare for them.

The problem with deciding to go to an event on the spur of the moment is that you don't get time to plan how to get the best out of it. For example, not so long ago we decided at short notice to go and see a show at the San Diego County Fair at Del Mar. We didn't leave until midday, and the traffic on the freeway was moving at a snail's pace. It was unbearable so we just turned around and went home. Spontaneity isn't always successful!

Making occasions special

If you've identified something to celebrate, or if you're planning an event that you want everyone to enjoy, how do you go about making it special? There's no point in putting a lot of effort into organising something that doesn't resonate with people or, worse, entails activities that they aren't comfortable with.

It's important to listen to what people have to say about their likes and dislikes, and the things that mean a lot to them. For example, planning a huge party for someone that would entail them having to make a speech to a room full of people would not be a kindness if they're the shy and retiring type. Getting this right requires paying attention to the little things that tell you about who someone is.

Picking up on cues

I was chatting to a friend about hiking in the Sierras, and he told me that one of his favourite family memories was hiking in Duck Pass as a kid. It was important to him because it was one of the few activities that he had shared with his father before he died. I'm determined to book that same trip and do it with him one day because I know it will be really special to him – this plan came simply from noticing how his eyes lit up when I mentioned hiking the Sierras.

TOP TIP

Even if you can't be present at someone's celebration, you can make the event special for them with a particularly well-chosen present. Again, it's about really listening to them, registering what they say and sending them something personal and relevant.

It doesn't have to be lavish

One of the most successful presents I have ever given was to a friend of mine in the UK who had bought a small speed boat and was so excited about taking it out to sea. I knew from experience that it can be tricky to find a spot to launch a boat from, so I searched the internet to see if there was a guide to boat-launching sites in northern England. There was one, but it was out of print, so I bought him a second-hand copy on eBay. My friend was delighted with it: the thought that had gone into this present more than made up for its cheapness.

The default position for celebrations often seems to be to throw money at them: to eat at a fancy restaurant, to go on a cruise or a holiday, to buy a lavish gift. There's nothing necessarily wrong with that – except that the more you spend, the bigger the disappointment if things don't go as planned.

CASE STUDY: Bonus blow-out

One of the best days out we've had recently was to celebrate me getting a big bonus at work. You would have thought that this would definitely be an occasion for big spending, but no. Instead, we went to the most extraordinary second-hand bookshop – they've got a shark sticking out of the bookshelf to mark the marine biology section – spent two happy hours browsing and bought eight books for $70. Then we went to a lovely place for a glass of wine. No excessive spending, just a unique experience and a relaxing day.

There are hundreds of ideas out there for how to make celebrations memorable without necessarily spending a lot of money. Ask others how they've marked everything from first birthdays to diamond wedding anniversaries, search the internet, have a rummage around in party stores – there's plenty of inspiration to be found. Others will appreciate the work that you've put in, and many will be happy to lend a hand.

The more you can personalise celebrations, the better. Someone I know of asked all the guests she invited to her wedding to send her a scrap of fabric from any unwanted clothes they had. She then used these scraps to make bunting to decorate the venue, but it also became a lasting souvenir of those who had helped her celebrate her big day.

Summary

Finding something to celebrate is the perfect way to break out of your routine. You don't have to stick to the established high days and holidays – get creative:

- Any occasion can be celebrated or commemorated, whether important or trivial, and turned into a special event.
- Local events are ideal for connecting and celebrating with your community.
- Diarising anniversaries and local activities will ensure you don't miss out.
- Picking up on cues from friends and family will enable you to organise personalised celebrations and presents that will mean a lot to them.

- You don't necessarily have to splash out to create a sense of occasion; celebrating on a shoestring can be just as much fun.

You've now got plenty of opportunities and ideas for turning an ordinary day into a memorable event, whatever the pretext. In the next chapter, we'll look at how to make the best use of the time you've managed to set aside – or carve out, even – so that not a moment is wasted.

FIVE
Making The Most Of Leisure

What a terrific day I'd had! I'd put in the groundwork organising my trip to Seattle, and it had definitely paid off. On my first day, I had:

- Wandered through underground Seattle on a brilliant walking tour through the ruins of the city after a fire in 1889, which had been built over in the decades that followed

- Visited the fantastic public food market and saw the fish tossing, where the stall holders just lob whole fish over the counter to whoever orders them

- Stopped off at the first-ever Starbucks coffee shop, with the original – more daring! – logo

- Explored the legendary Seattle Aquarium
- Browsed the curios in Ye Olde Curiosity Shop (established 1899)
- Chowed down on a steaming clam chowder down on the pier
- Relaxed on a boat trip around the bay, discovering its history and the industries that surround it

I had scheduled everything perfectly, starting off with the 'big rocks' like the aquarium and the tour of the bay, and then filling in the spaces between them with pebbles like visiting the public market and the original Starbucks. I plotted a route that would allow me to take in as much as possible but without having to rush, and making sure that I arrived at all the attractions at the best time: not too crowded, not just about to close up. Checking whether there were any stand-out places to eat near where I was going was another good move.

This being Seattle, there was still plenty to see and do over the next few days, not least the monorail, the space needle, the Jimi Hendrix museum, a trip on a sea plane, and lots more. I would have to plan the next day just as well to ensure I got the most out of my trip.

Catch the day

When on holiday, there is nothing to match the satisfaction of knowing you've made good use of your time and seen as much as possible of the attractions on offer. However, that doesn't happen without careful planning, both of the event or activity itself, and in choosing – and securing – the right time for it.

In the earlier chapters we looked at the importance of ringfencing leisure time in the face of all efforts to encroach on it. However, when it comes to getting time off work, a lot will depend on the type of organisation you work in and your position in it. I learned the hard way about the importance of thinking ahead: for years I ended up working at Christmas and Easter, and on other public holidays I was always the one holding the fort. It took me a long time to get myself organised enough to look at my calendar and think things through.

You also need to think about your teammates, though, especially those with family commitments. You should encourage them to plan ahead too, and warn them that you are about to arrange leave dates and make travel plans that could see them lose out unless they stake their claim. If your dates have been approved, it's hard for colleagues to come along later and challenge them. It can be like *Hunger Games* in the office, a race to secure the dates early to bag the vacation!

If instead you can set up a civilised negotiation with colleagues, it will avoid a lot of resentment.

As part of your planning, it's vital to take into account the obvious but often overlooked factor of the weather. (Much as I still love the UK, I can't recommend visiting there in the winter – a lot of your time will be spent in darkness!) You won't be able to enjoy sightseeing and sports activities, for example, if you're not properly dressed. There's nothing more miserable than feeling too cold to appreciate a visit somewhere and having to cut it short because you need to warm up. Thanks to Google, you can find out the average daytime and night-time temperatures of most places at any given time of year. Remember though, just because you're visiting somewhere hot doesn't mean that you will have no need for any warm clothing. Over-airconditioned museums and chilly caves can be just as uncomfortable. (For what it's worth, I recommend a thin, Patagonia-type jacket: not bulky, flexible and warm when you zip it up.)

Remember that many places have a specific 'season', and if you visit them outside of that period, no matter how good the weather, you may find restaurants, bars and attractions are closed. It's worth checking up on 'shoulder seasons', which are the transitional periods between high and low season – things may be cheaper, but check whether attractions have more limited opening times.

Dovetailing

If you have limited leave available, look for opportunities for what the French call 'making a bridge': those occasions when public holidays fall in such a way that if you add just one day of leave, you can get four days off in a row. For example, if the days fall right over Christmas and New Year, you can get ten days off in a row by adding in three days of your leave allowance.

You could also look to combine work and leisure. If you have a work trip somewhere interesting that is not going to take the whole day, don't rush back to the office. Why not book half a day's leave to explore the area?

CASE STUDY: Making a day of it

It can be quite a drive from my home in San Diego to Los Angeles, so when I had to meet a vendor at a Lakers game, I also took some time off to get the best out of the trip. I went on a tour of the Getty Villa's gardens, ate at the 'best burger' joint in the city, and took in the Warner Brothers Studio Tour, which was amazing. Oh, and I almost got killed by a homeless pirate ninja in the car park – it was certainly an exciting trip!

Even on an ordinary work day, you can seek out opportunities for a break from routine, depending on where you work. A quick visit to a nearby museum is easy to fit in, but even just eating somewhere new or sitting in the park can recharge your batteries. If you practise a version of the Pomodoro method of parcelling up time that I described in Chapter Two, it should be easy to identify blocks of time that you can give over to a refreshing change of scene and routine.

Getting out of your own office space to see what some of your more remote colleagues are doing is also enjoyable. As I said in Chapter Three, it's a great way of connecting with people, but it could also be a chance to discover more about how your organisation functions, get insight into a totally different sort of work, and just generally break out of the 'same old same old'. To be honest, I'd rather go on an impromptu interoffice visit than a team Christmas dinner any day.

It's perhaps harder to think of opportunities if your workplace is the home, and there are some domestic chores that it's probably impossible to inject any fun into (cleaning the bathroom?). However, even so, there are opportunities to be found. For example, if you are a person who does ironing, that's a chance to catch up on soaps or movies you may have missed, or listen to any audio books you want to hit.

It can also help if you gamify tasks: one minute to remove every toy from the floor, or ten minutes to identify ten unused bits of junk cluttering your house that can be taken to the thrift store. Keeping the time you spend on these activities to a minimum adds up to more leisure time for meeting up with a friend for a coffee, or reading a book.

> **TOP TIP**
>
> Your family will remember the event you all went to together; they won't remember that the bathroom was a bit messier the following day because you skipped cleaning it to go on the outing.

I'm also keen on making plans for midweek activities, as this saves your weekends for the big pay-off trips. Anything that only takes two or three hours is ideal to squeeze in midweek: the theatre, movies, perhaps an evening event at a gallery where they may also be serving drinks and/or hosting a talk. These are also the sorts of activities that I like to do with a friend, meaning I can save my weekends for my family

Doing things on a budget

Getting the best out of your leisure time doesn't have to be expensive (though conversely, you can make even the simplest pastime expensive if you want to). As I mentioned before, where you can, booking things out of season is a good way to make savings (and you may well find your destination a lot less crowded, which is always a bonus).

At any given time, there will be discounts on fares and attractions on offer. Keeping an eye open for them and asking around to find out how others have accessed them is always a good idea. When I couldn't find a route between San Diego and Montana that wasn't long and expensive, I asked a colleague who had family there for advice. 'Easy,' she said, 'get a cheap flight to Las Vegas and a "puddle jumper" the rest of the way.' Standby theatre tickets cost much less than those booked in advance, and many attractions slash their entry fees in the last hour before they close. In Chapter Seven we'll look in more detail at the travel discounts on offer and who is eligible.

CASE STUDY: Africa for free

When I worked at Vodafone, Lynn was one of the sales team supports. She was planning to get married and have children, but she wanted some adventure before she did so. She didn't earn a great deal, so just booking a holiday somewhere exotic was not an option.

She began researching how to go on holiday for free and discovered a charity that offered opportunities for volunteer work if you paid double the actual cost of the trip. Our company said they would match half the cost of the trip, so she only had to pay $1,500.

She proceeded to raise that amount herself through organising activities for her sales team – for example, sweepstakes where half the money collected constituted the prize, and the other half went towards her travel kitty. She was relentless: there was something different on every week. Full marks for persistence.

Needless to say, she raised all the money she needed, went to Africa, took part in the volunteering activities and generally had a wild time.

The key lesson here is to get creative. Many activities represent opportunities for a company to fulfil their social engagement aims, so you may be able to find a win-win all round.

Think local

Museums and galleries often have special discounts, or even free sessions for local residents, so it's worth finding out when these are coming up.

Volunteering opportunities often come with perks, such as free tickets. The ushers at our local theatre, for example, get to use the tickets of people who don't turn up for shows or sit in on performances after the curtain has gone up. Volunteering to help people with disabilities enjoy their leisure time by accompanying them to theatres, movies or galleries also gets you free entry – and the chance to connect with new people whom you otherwise may not have come into contact with.

> **CASE STUDY: To the stars and beyond**
>
> I studied astronomy in the UK, but it didn't involve much practical use of telescopes, and anyway it was cloudy most of the time in Plymouth. However, I still

really wanted to use a large telescope. These sorts of telescopes don't come cheap, and I didn't want to invest in something that I wasn't sure I'd be able to use correctly. I discovered that one evening a month our local IMAX cinema is taken over by an amateur astronomy club, and they have a visiting professor come to give a lecture. As a bonus, afterwards, a few of the members bring out their telescopes and are keen to get new people interested in their hobby. I got to see Jupiter and Saturn in incredible detail, picked up some fantastic information from enthusiastic experts – and met some kind and knowledgeable people!

When it comes to festivals, not many people know that they are spoiled for choice. Everyone has heard of the carnival in Venice or Rio, but there are probably hundreds out there within easy reach of you, however niche your interests: foodie festivals, vintage fairs, veteran cars, you name it. One of the most successful family events we ever went to was the Thomas the Tank Engine Festival put on by a railway and aircraft museum an hour's drive from us. What's more, you can often get free tickets to festivals if you volunteer to help with stewarding or litter-picking afterwards, for example.

Doubling up

Combining activities can also be a good way of saving money. For example, going to see a show and then out for dinner afterwards can work out to be expensive, but if you book a show that includes dinner, you could save a fortune. When my mother visited from the UK, one of the best activities we did was to go and have lunch 'with' killer whales at a marine attraction where you get to eat right next to the aquarium and learn all about them from marine biologists.

CASE STUDY: Who dun it?

I'd heard good things about a murder mystery night in Las Vegas and booked to go with my family. We were seated close to the stage, had a great dinner, and Jake was thrilled to be selected to go up on stage as part of the band and play guitar. At the end, the inspector came in to solve the mystery and announced that the murderer was a young person who was being quiet and lying low, and for a terrifying moment Jake thought it was going to be him. Imagine his relief when a young woman was denounced, and rushed up on stage brandishing a fake gun.

We couldn't stop laughing and still talk about it now, which I don't think we'd be doing if it had just been a meal.

Doubling up can also mean sharing the costs. Booking a hotel as an individual or a couple can leave your pockets empty, but if the occasion involves meeting up with a number of other people, jointly renting a cottage – a villa or a mansion, even – costs far less per head and gives you access to much better accommodation than you might otherwise be able to afford.

Going back to my trip to climb the Half Dome, I halved the cost by inviting my colleague along and sharing the expense of the petrol and the hotels. (It also halved the strain of the ten-hour drive, and definitely doubled the fun!)

Summary

Our leisure time is precious, so it pays to plan to get the most out of it.

- It's vital to think ahead when organising your leisure time. For most people that means getting in early with booking time off work – but also sparing a thought for the needs of your colleagues.

- Do factor the weather into your planning – the English simile 'a face like a wet weekend' perfectly expresses the depressing effect of poor weather on holiday…

- Look for opportunities to extend your leisure time through creative use of public holidays, or combining periods of leisure into any travel you have to do for work.

- Make the most of the free activities your community has to offer, and of any discounts available to you through your age or status, for example.

- Sharing costs with friends or family is a great way to afford things that would be beyond your price range on your own, such as renting high-end accommodation.

There is a definite art to making the most of leisure time, so in the next chapter we'll be getting into the finer points of planning and looking at some tools that can help you with this.

SIX
Planning

Here is my to-do list for 2025:

- Rodeo at Petco Park – Jan
- Venture Scouts with Jake – Jan
- Mesa Rim Climbing with Laurie – Jan
- MotorCross Snapdragon Stadium – Jan
- Plays at local theatres in '25 – put provisional dates in for the year
- Fast in January with Rock Church – Jan
- Spa day for wife's birthday – Jan
- Nine holes at SailHo with Tony – Jan
- Deadline for Jake's college applications – Jan

GET A LIFE

- Pickleball lessons with Laurie – Jan
- Drive-In Theatre Oceanside – Feb
- Hungry Dog 5K run with pet – Feb
- Hikes – Cowles Mountain in Feb, Iron Mountain in Feb
- Skiing with Dave in Denver – Feb
- Sign up for CISSP 90-day exam prep class – Feb
- Rent a Sprinter van for the weekend – Feb
- Get green ink for St Patrick's Day – Mar
- Viking Festival in North Carolina – Mar
- Planetarium with Jake – Mar
- Strikeforce Arena football season opener – Mar
- A different indoor climbing spot with Laurie – Apr
- Big Bear weekend – Apr
- Renfair Escondido – Apr
- Revisit inheritance, gift and tax planning – Apr
- Mount Vernon in North Carolina, Revolutionary War reenactment weekend – May
- Gator by the Bay – May
- Temecula Balloon and Wine Festival – May
- Sit CISSP exam – May
- Bay Bridge run – May

PLANNING

- Memphis family trip – May
- Jake's graduation – May
- Deadline for permits for Yosemite and rim-to-rim hike – 26 May
- Rock-n-Roll half marathon – Jun
- Mud Run at Marine Base in Camp Pendleton – Jun
- Jake and Laurie to Catalina Scout camp for diving badge – Jun
- Jake's eighteenth birthday, driving at the track day – Jun
- Wedding anniversary at Viva Las Vegas, renew vows with Elvis – Jun
- Utah Shakespeare, six-play festival – Jun
- Gettysburg reenactment for Fourth of July weekend
- Take kayak out – Jul
- Renew Jake's British passport, summer project – Jul
- Boogie boarding with Jake – Jul
- Jetboat with Andre/Tony – Jul
- Star Trek Convention in Las Vegas – Aug
- England trip with Jake and Laurie for a week – Aug
- Huntington Beach Civil War reenactment – Aug

- Cooking class with Laurie on homemade pasta – Sep
- Painting: have one submitted to the Watercolour Museum – Sep
- Yosemite via Fresno airport, long weekend / week – Sep
- Octoberfest – Oct
- Rim-to-Rim hike in Arizona – Oct
- Safari Park with Laurie and Jake – Oct
- Renfair in Houston (biggest in America) – Oct
- Sequoia weekend – Oct
- 'Ride the Point' bike ride – Nov
- K1 go karting with Jake – Nov
- Savannah and Charleston trip for Thanksgiving weekend – Nov
- Escape room, easy level, date night with Laurie – Dec
- Oil Painting class date night – Dec
- Getty Museum day trip with Jake – Dec
- Christmas in Chicago with Laurie's parents – Dec
- Business book: publish *Get A Life* (!)

If you think the above looks like a jumbled mess, you'd be absolutely right. This is just a way of capturing all the events and aspirations before you start planning for real.

So how do you turn what looks like a rather random selection of holiday suggestions, ideas for outings, notes to self, project proposals and vague timelines into an actionable plan? The methods I will run through in this chapter work for me, and could work for you, whether you are a pen and paper person, fully digital or something in between. For example, post-it notes are great for helping you to sequence ideas quickly, and you can either photograph the results, or key them in for cutting and pasting in future.

Keep a list

The importance of a list can be summed up in this simple equation: no list = FOMO. I have a list (something like the above) of all the events, activities and projects I have in mind for a year, showing the months in which they occur or when I want them to be completed. This 'master list' is key: this is your go-to spot for checking what is coming up and transferring it to your calendar, planner or Outlook. The diagram/illustration of my calendar below shows how this works, with long-term events from my annual/quarterly planner (as featured in Chapter One) transferred in alongside the informal, ad hoc events that arise, such as a dentist visit, which you don't want to book in only to find it clashes with something that's taken a long time to arrange. The example below was my birthday month, so perhaps not typical, but exceptions to the routine are the aim of the game.

29 Mon	30 Tues	31 Weds	1 Thurs
Gwendal in town from Singapore, meet up and drinks			Dentist for crown
5	**6**	**7**	**8**
12	**13**	**14**	**15**
			Team lunch at California English with auditors
19	**20**	**21**	**22**
Dave's in town from Denver Take Dave to burrito spot to sample SD culture	Off-site meeting at Marcelo's house	Team building night at Junction Bar & Grill	Home for new washing machine delivery
26	**27**	**28**	**29**
		Cooking lesson date night with Chef Laura – French bistro theme	51st birthday!! Denver Dinner at Prado, Henry VI Parts 2/3 at Old Globe

August in my calendar

2 Fri	3 Sat	4 Sun
Art Walk preview night – look for Richard Oliver	La Jolla Theatre play: 'Please Don't Dress for Dinner'	
9	**10**	**11**
JetSki Catalina – Long Beach with Tony		Date night with Laurie at Stone Brewery
16	**17**	**18**
Dave's in town from Denver		
Offshore fishing trip with Dave, fish and chips at Shakespeare's pub	Tour of San Onofre Nuclear Power Station and bike ride	America's Finest City Half Marathon with Dave, and Phill's BBQ
23	**24**	**25**
	Family dinner out at Presley's and play: Ms Holmes & Ms Watson, Old Globe Theatre	Bike the Bay with Laurie – 25-mile ride across Coronado ridge
30	**31**	**1**
Family trip to Big Bear		
Gateway Diner for lunch, tour of Big Bear		Hike with family and dog, more board games and drive home

Whenever you notice that you've missed out on a seasonal or annual/recurring activity, add it to your list for next time. Very quickly your leisure time for the next year will begin to take shape. I love having that great tapestry of events and excitement to look forward to. The other big advantage of this method is that it gives you somewhere to record the actions that you need to take in advance if your plans are to come to fruition. For example, if you want to go for a hike in a national park in October, you probably need to apply for the visa to do so in May. If you are that way inclined and need to manage a complex project such as a big family event where you need to coordinate the travel and accommodation of a lot of people, you could probably do this using a Gantt chart.

The other thing to note about the master list is that the entries in it fall into different categories. Mine are:

- Personal development goals – for example, running times, books to read
- Home improvement projects – new door for lounge
- Travel and holiday proposals – trip to Pasadena, visit to UK
- Adventure goals – sailing day, diving in a kelp forest
- Family activities – board games to play, movies to watch together

- Admin projects – renew Jake's passport, consolidate pensions
- Activities for Jake – scouting badges, building a robot

Some entries will need their own page – for example, you'll definitely need one for planning a complex trip.

Digital or paper?

Where you maintain your list is a matter of personal choice. For the past thirteen years I've been using the back pages of my planner – I like having a hard copy of my lists and calendar to hand. Recently I've been experimenting with Microsoft's One Note, which works well, and many people I know use the Notes app on their phone, or Google Sheets, to keep similar records.

There are a whole variety of paper-based planners out there. I use a Moleskine XL Monthly View, and I've been advising others to use it too. At the time of writing it costs $39.99, and what I love about it is that you can divide up the space at the front into quarters and document your progress; use the monthly views to plan vacation dates and flag up birthdays; and keep the space at the back for notes, building your master list for the next year, and generally being your second brain.

Moleskine do a huge range of notebooks and planners, some with habit trackers or folders at the back for keeping any documentation you might need, and they have even introduced a 'smart notebook' where what you write in it using the accompanying smart pen appears simultaneously in the Notes app on your phone.

I don't have shares in Moleskine, honest! There are lots of other brands available; Leuchtturm and Rhodia notebooks are also great.

TOP TIP

A good master list is likely to be based on a number of supporting lists that capture your ideas as you go along. Looking back at old planners I can see that I've compiled lists of date night ideas, purchase wish lists, courses to consider, and present lists (backed up with lists of presents already given so I can avoid duplication!).

Your list needs to be a live document that you are constantly updating. If you notice an event, or you have a great idea about an event you'd like to organise or an activity you'd like to try, write it down or record it on your phone immediately, or email it to yourself. Too many times a great idea has come to me, but by the time I've got back to my desk a couple of hours later I've forgotten all about it.

You can't do everything, but if you note it in the moment, you can at least research it, decide whether you want to do it, and write it down or write it off. This means that if, say, someone mentions the Christmas parade of lights (an annual event in San Diego when boat owners festoon their boats in lights and cruise round the bay) is on this weekend and you note it down as something you might like to do, even if you can't make it this year, you'll be able to plan for it next year.

This is your list to add to, annotate or take away from as you wish, but you obviously need to share the bits of it that affect others with the people in question. If you know that March is a good time to go for a day's skiing trip in Big Bear (because that's the cheap shoulder period), make sure you share this information with your skiing friends well in advance.

As you can't do everything, and events may clash, part of the process of listing involves prioritising, whether on the basis of the things that are most important to you, or on what's going to fit in with your other upcoming commitments. You will be left with a shorter list of things to do over the next three to six months, but now that you have a system, you can transfer anything that's been dropped for this year over to next year.

CASE STUDY: A starter list

If the prospect of launching straight into a grand master list for activities a year or maybe even two in advance is a bit daunting, try mapping out the next three to six months. An achievable list of events could look something like this:

- 15 March: Mother's birthday – book table at [name of restaurant]
- 3 April: Easter Parade through city centre
- 10 May: Day's hiking in national park (remember to buy US topographical map)
- 1 June: Invites to neighbours for Independence Day barbecue
- 12 June: Wine tasting session at vineyard
- 4 July: Lunchtime, barbecue with neighbours/evening, fireworks over harbour

Sources of information

The internet has made the world your oyster. All attractions have their own website, and many offer advice on planning your visit and creating an itinerary. Google Maps can help you find restaurants and other attractions in the area so that you can get the most out of a day, and you can also use Google to search for other people's itineraries for particular locations. I've also discovered and started using smarter search engines, such as Bing's Co-pilot, which is powered by Chat GPT. It gave me a great suggested itinerary for a four-bookshop tour in New York, based on the places I said I wanted to see.

TripAdvisor can be a useful source of information as people often include helpful itineraries that they've worked out ('Here's an idea for a five-day trip to New Orleans'), or flag up hidden gems that they've discovered while visiting somewhere (such as the Jurassic Technology Museum in LA).

A word of warning though: don't disappear down a research rabbit hole. It's all too easily done, as many of these sites can be seductive. The law of diminishing returns definitely applies here: there is no point in continuing to research something if the same details keep coming up.

Guidebooks are great, but of course they're bulky and go out of date. Most guidebook publishers also have online versions of their guides, which are updated regularly by whole armies of contributors. Having said that, one type of guidebook that I've found particularly useful is the slim-enough-to-fit-into-a-pocket Dorling Kindersley Top Ten guides. They're great when you're visiting a new country or city and have limited time.

There is a list of useful resources in the back of the book, and you will probably be able to add your own local resources to that list.

Mailing lists

It's essential to get on the mailing lists of the events and venues that you want to go to. Not only does this ensure that you'll always get reminders for anything you're interested in but, in many cases, you'll get priority booking, meaning that you'll be able to book ahead of the general public and may be in line for discounts as well. Some organisations operate these mailing lists on a membership basis, so you might have to pay an annual fee, but this will be more than offset by discounts on tickets.

Here's a sample of the mailing lists that I'm on:

- **Sports**
    - Baseball: San Diego (SD) Padres (best stadium in the world, and food stalls from the city's iconic restaurants)
    - Soccer: SD Loyal (men's team) and SD Wave (women's team) at the Snapdragon Stadium
    - Ice hockey: SD Gulls at the Sports Arena (not forgetting Phil's Barbecue)
    - Lacrosse: SD Seals

- **Local events**
    - SD Bayfair: Powerboat racing in Mission Bay
    - SD Restaurant Week: Restaurants offer bite-sized portions of the best dishes – a great night out as you try many different cuisines in a single stroll

- SD Fleet Week: A variety of events across the city to support the military and their families
- Balboa Park December Nights: Food, music and events in the run-up to Christmas
- SD Old Town Fiesta Cinco de Mayo: A celebration of Mexican culture and heritage
- Gator by the Bay: A lively festival featuring Cajun, Zydeco and blues music
- La Jolla Music Society Summerfest: A month-long chamber music festival
- Parade of Lights: The boating community in SD light up their boats and parade through the bay for two weekends every December

You should be able to build something similar for your location, depending on your interests. You might also want to add theatres, museums and concert halls, and children's events.

Work backwards

Some activities entail a lot more planning than others. Pretty much all you have to do for a trip to the movies is buy tickets and turn up on time. However, for activities that involve more people, more travel, perhaps documentation, vaccinations and weather considerations, there is a lot more to think about than simply booking the activity itself.

GET A LIFE

CASE STUDY: Shakespeare in Utah

An opportunity to do something we've always wanted to do has suddenly opened up. I've spotted on my planner that my partner's leave coincides with the Shakespeare Festival in Utah, which has been on my master list for a couple of years. If I book four days' leave, we can make the most of the festival week.

It's not just a question of booking the tickets, though. Getting to southern Utah is a challenge in itself, because there are no direct flights. It'll mean a flight to Salt Lake City, and then a puddle jumper down to Cedar City. Then of course there's the car rental and the accommodation – and that's before you even think about the tickets for plays, talks and activities...

Take hiking the Grand Canyon's rim-to-rim trail. You need to think about the best time of year to go, get everyone in the party to coordinate their leave (Calendly or Doodle can help you here), put in for the permit lottery, get in early with your campsite bookings (which cannot be done more than three months in advance, so you have to jump in as soon as the booking window opens) and so on. This means that planning for an event that is to take place in October needs to start in February. If you don't take this far-sighted approach and work backwards, you can guarantee that either you will be disappointed, or you will have to pay way over the odds to make up for your lack of foresight.

If theatre or the opera are your thing, make sure you get onto the mailing list of the companies you're interested in, so that you can be quick off the mark when their bookings open. Adding a note in your calendar to remind you to book on the opening day will prompt you to put that task in your personal daily or weekly to-do-list when the date rolls round. To make the task even easier, add any relevant information or links to save yourself time. Take the Gator by the Bay crawfish event: the exact date for next year is not yet confirmed, but a reminder and a link to its site appear in my calendar six months beforehand, when the event's website will have been updated and all the details have become available.

No such thing as overpreparation

Even once you've got the booking and the logistics down to a fine art, you may have more preparation to do. For any outdoorsy trip, you need to think about equipment. Shoes are the most basic piece of equipment: if you haven't got the right ones, a day's walking or hiking can be a disaster. Never venture forth in boots you haven't worn before and know to be comfortable. For that trip in October, you probably need to start breaking in a new pair of boots from July – three months is about right, as you don't want to wear them down or crush the compression pad from overuse.

GET A LIFE

TOP TIP

For what it's worth, my advice is to get walking boots that won't let your ankle roll: 80% of injuries happen when people are going back down the mountain because they're tired, and you don't want to have to pay out for being flown out of the Sierras!

Likewise, check your camping equipment. You can't expect to dump it in a garage and bring it out a year later, all in perfect order with no holes and batteries still fully charged. Again, if you have new equipment, test it out beforehand and get familiar with it. You don't want to be struggling to erect an unfamiliar tent in the pouring rain after a 20-mile hike.

CASE STUDY: Taking the veil

It was a good thing I read the AllTrails review before we hiked to Duck Pass. I had bought a mosquito net for each member of the family, so when we hit a 2-mile stretch of the trail that was thick with mosquitos we just wrapped ourselves in our nets and marched confidently through, coming out the other end untouched. Many people we met later that day were covered in bites, which had put a dampener on the rest of their excursion.

And you – are you in perfect working order? You need to be up to the challenges you've set yourself. When I climbed the Half Dome with my friend Daniel, he wasn't taking any chances. For about a year beforehand he would go down to the San Diego convention centre every weekend with a full backpack and train by running up and down the external stairs, which are at least three storeys high.

It's a good idea to have one or more dry runs for a big physical excursion, just as marathon runners build up with half marathons, so you know where the pitfalls are and have worked out how to get round them.

Delisting

Remember, you are in charge of your list; it isn't in charge of you. It's perfectly OK to take things off your list. This is another reason why dry runs are such a good idea. Suppose you've done a mini camping trip in preparation for a longer one. If you haven't enjoyed it, couldn't sleep and found the alfresco toilet arrangements a bit much, it's unlikely you'll fare any better on the full trip and might want to reconsider if that's something you really want to do.

Other list items that you might want to question are those that keep getting carried over from year to year. The fact that they never seem to become a priority should tell you something. I must admit there are a few of these on my list: the Gator by the Bay crawfish festival and a family city break to Boston are two examples, but one I've finally removed from my list is a trip to the Rainbow Falls at Mammoth, in the Sierras. It's a seven-hour drive each way, and each time the opportunity has come up we just haven't been able to face it. After three years of deferring it, I had to be honest that I didn't want it badly enough. Think what you could do with fourteen hours not spent behind the wheel!

The proactive approach can become addictive, and you may find you have been overdoing it. You will know when this happens, because you'll wake up one morning, look at your calendar and say to yourself, 'Do I really want to do X, Y or Z tonight?' and decide that actually you don't. You've overcommitted, but you probably couldn't have known you were going to – that's fine.

The only exception to delisting is when you have made a commitment to someone else. If I've planned to take my son boogie boarding, I'll stick with the plan even if I don't particularly want to go. I'll also always follow through on arrangements I've made with friends.

The whole point of proactive personal planning is to improve your quality of life, so it would be madness to let it become a straitjacket forcing you into things you don't want to do.

Summary

Fulfilling leisure events don't arise spontaneously. You need to put in a bit of effort to make them happen.

PLANNING

- First and foremost, you need to make a list. If you take only one thing away from this book, make sure it's this. A master list is key.

- Your list can be in any format you like: digital, in a notebook, in a loose-leaf folder – whatever works for you.

- If a year-long master list is a bit daunting, draw up a starter list of activities and events that seem do-able.

- The internet is a treasure trove, but don't overlook local sources of information such as libraries and other community resources.

- When it comes to planning more complicated trips, work backwards to ensure you're covering all the necessary bases, such as visas, inoculations, etc.

- There is no such thing as overpreparation.

- You're allowed to take things off your list if you change your mind or find it's not a priority.

Now you've done the basic planning, it's time to move up a level to one of the most demanding elements of successful trips: travel, with all its joys, pitfalls and unsuspected challenges.

SEVEN
Travel

The scribbles below were the starting point for a fantastic trip to Wales with the family, taking in castles, museums and some fabulous scenery.

I started off by searching for hotels on Expedia and Google and reading their TripAdvisor reviews, booking them from the US. I looked up the opening times and the prices for all the locations and figured out the driving times between them, to get to my final itinerary. Most of the tickets for attractions and sites I bought when I turned up at the location, so as to get maximum flexibility on the day in case our plans needed to change.

GET A LIFE

Planning a trip to Wales

We set off for Cardiff from my mum's house in Hampshire, stopping off in Bath to watch my brother Tony conduct his first guided tour of the city for tourists – after thirty years in the police service. Then we crossed the River Severn and promptly got lost because my nephew's satnav wasn't letting us take any motorways; we kept getting turned away from the bridge until we figured this out… Nevertheless, we made it to Cardiff, did a tour and had dinner.

On day two we took in Cardiff Castle and the National Museum Cardiff, then hit the road again to Snowdonia.

On day three we visited Caernarfon Castle, the Big Pit National Coal Museum and Conwy Castle.

It was great fun, but at times Jake found it all a bit much and began moaning. On day three I realised he'd had enough and offered him the choice of staying the night in a hotel or doing the 4-hour drive back to granny's house. He opted for the trip back to granny's and promised not to complain the whole journey – a promise he kept, and he was rewarded with vast amounts of ice cream for his patience.

As this experience demonstrates, planning travel for a group of people, even a small group, calls for lots of attention to detail in terms of the nuts and bolts of logistics and bookings, but also tactical adjustments all the way along to accommodate everyone's tolerance (or not) for inconvenience, queuing, long hours in a car and so forth. Recognising when you have reached the point of diminishing returns and beating a retreat before your companions – or you – lose the will to live is vital. Once you've got all you can out of a trip, it's probably not wise to try to squeeze in one more attraction.

Timetables

Timetables are the bedrock of successful travel planning, but some are more useful than others. Unless you have plenty of time on your hands and infinite patience, you'll usually want to go for the fastest transport option with the fewest changes.

Airlines

Each airline has its own website, but the websites that show a range of flights, like Expedia, Skyscanner and Google Flights, have the advantage of offering a price comparison, so that you can trade off between convenience and price. For example, I discovered that you could get a super-cheap flight to the US from the UK – provided you were happy to make a stop-off in New Zealand, which would take the total duration of travel to two-and-a-half days. The reasoning here is that an occupied seat is better than an empty one, so airlines are keen to fill lightly booked flights. In general, though, I would always favour a more direct flight, simply because it reduces the possibility of disruption.

CASE STUDY: Nightmare journey

I once got stuck at San Francisco airport with Jake when he was just nine months old (my wife was travelling for work). We were there for nine hours rather than three because a storm kept delaying our departure. What made things worse was that Jake had an ear infection and was really suffering, the poor little mite. The gate agent desk was besieged with distressed passengers, and we were lucky to get the last flight out. Others were having to accept flights on the following day for destinations miles from their home.

Then they wouldn't let me take Jake's bottle through customs so I had to source more baby formula in an airport not designed around babies. Needless to say, the formula I had to buy was so different from what he was used to that he ended up even more miserable. That was one bumpy ride!

The moral of the above story is to avoid hub cities if you can, and especially hub cities that are renowned for bad weather, such as San Francisco or Chicago. (LA, on the other hand, has perfect weather all year round!)

Another thing you need to be aware of when booking is any time difference, but thankfully these can all be checked on your mobile. Unhelpfully, the changeover from daylight saving to ordinary time takes place on different dates in different countries and even between states in the US, so take care if you are booking ahead for late March or October dates.

Accept all offers of updates being sent to your phone. They may turn out to be mostly unnecessary, but it's worth putting up with the annoyance just so you don't miss that vital notification telling you about the change of terminal for your flight in three hours' time.

Package deals

Although combined flight and hotel packages are not generally on offer in the US, they are a great option if you are planning an extended trip to Europe. They represent good value for money, and although they often include group tours, you are not obliged to go on them. If you're not choosy about where you want to stay, these packages could be the cheapest way to get to your chosen destination; once you're there, you can follow your own itinerary.

Trains and buses

Timetables for most local trains and buses are now available online, which helps a lot with planning the finer details of journeys both in the US and abroad. The main drawback with these timetables is that they may state that there is a reduced service on 'feast days', without telling you which days those are. As a local you would know; as a traveller, you could be caught out. This is where the local tourist information office comes in useful (see below), or you could consult www.timeanddate.com, which lists public holidays alphabetically by country.

Booking

One of the most annoying things about booking travel is the wide price range for any given journey. Everyone knows that peak times are more expensive than off-peak or low seasons, but if you have school-age children in your group, you just have to hold your nose while somehow managing to pay through it.

Getting a deal

Even so, the point at which you make the booking can make a difference and prevent paying over the odds. The difficulty is that the 'best' booking periods tend to move around, to the point where it's hard to keep up. Most companies have systems by which they offer price reductions for early bookings, and then some deals are available at the last minute, with the period in between being the most expensive, but as consumers get wise to these patterns and begin to exploit them more efficiently, the companies tend to move the goal posts. That said, you can sign up for price alerts for flights, hotels and trains; the 'Resources' section at the back of the book lists the main sources of information. If you have a credit card registered with an airline, you will also receive alerts about sales or discounts.

Google Flights and Expedia are handy tools for finding out more travel information, but you can't beat asking around your friends, colleagues and family to see if anyone has done a similar trip before and can offer advice.

Even if you don't manage to catch that elusive cheap booking date, there are many other ways to get discounted travel and accommodation, and thankfully they don't require you to be checking your calendar or emails all the time.

If you qualify, membership of the American Association of Retired Persons (AARP) can get you reductions on a number of things. I joined for $10 a year when I turned fifty, to get $10 a month off my phone bill – a win-win. Similarly, the American Automobile Association (AAA) offers discounts on a wide range of activities and products, again, not all of them travel related.

Students will also often qualify for travel discounts, which colleges should be able to advise on, and there are sizeable discounts on offer for essential workers such as first responders, healthcare professionals and the military, so it's worth checking whether you are entitled to any concessions. I would also recommend checking out www.thepointsguy.com for more travel savings and rewards tips.

Car rental

My wife is the queen of car rental, as she travels so much for work. We use every type of discount, from the one that comes with our AAA membership to the points that come with credit cards and loyalty rewards from extensive travel. The big cost risk with rental cars is if they get damaged. To be sure you are not hit with any claims for damage to the car, don't forget to take photos of the exterior and the interior before you drive it away, so that you have evidence in case of a dispute.

Accommodation

Whatever type of accommodation you have in mind – hotels, Airbnb, camping – the cardinal rule is to always read the reviews before booking. What seems too good to be true probably is. We found this out to our cost when we booked a cheap and central hotel in San Francisco – only to find it was in the middle of contested gangland territory in the Tenderloin district, an area so scary even the cops don't go down there. If we'd read the reviews from people who had made the same mistake as we had (which are hysterical, by the way) we'd have steered well clear of it.

Packing

Successful packing is a fine art, but with practice you will become an expert. Sometimes it seems there's no happy medium between spending your whole trip shivering or roasting and wishing you'd brought smarter/more casual/more practical clothes, or getting back from your trip and realising you've been carting around a ton of stuff that you never ended up wearing.

Every holiday season there's no end of advice online and in papers and fashion magazines, and I wouldn't aim to compete with them in the style stakes. However, from a practical standpoint, these are my guidelines:

- Go for neutral colours that will mix and match well.

- A lightweight jacket that will keep you warm yet can be stowed away in a small space is essential – the Patagonia jacket fits the bill (known as PataGucci in the active sports industry).

- All-black trainers are the perfect multitaskers. They can pass for shoes in more formal situations, but they'll be comfortable for walking long distances.

- Likewise, black jeans can pass for business smart casual – but don't wear them in hot climates unless you want roasted thighs!

- If you are going camping, or on a longer trip, make sure you have clothing that dries quickly – nothing kills the appetite for exploration like having to put on a damp sweatshirt.

TOP TIP

If you are travelling with children, make a comprehensive list of what you will need and check – twice – that you have packed everything. You don't want to discover at 30,000 feet that your offspring's cherished cuddly toy has failed to make the flight...

For the same reason, search the hotel room or apartment in minute detail before you leave, to spare yourself screams and heartache later. Remember that infants spend a lot of time on the floor, so look under beds, tables and chairs for toys that have gone AWOL.

What you pack everything in is a matter of personal preference, and you can roughly divide people up according to whether they are soft or hard luggage fans. Just avoid cheap luggage, because it's bound to fall apart on you at the most inconvenient moment. By contrast, don't waste your money on expensive luggage, because if you take the advice in this book to heart, you'll find that it won't be long before your luggage starts to look a bit battered. Something robust and reasonable that you won't mind getting a few scuffs and knocks on (it's got to survive baggage handlers and aircraft holds) is ideal. Don't get something that weighs a ton before you've even put anything into it.

I personally prefer a wheelie bag. After years of travelling round the world with a thirty- or forty-litre backpack, I realised the madness of it: the sweaty back, the weight bouncing around as you rush for the gate, the straps cutting into your shoulders – never again.

Finally, when travelling with children, you can forget all about travelling light. Check in as much as you can. You may still end up carrying four bags, a car seat and a baby down the aisle of a plane and clipping every single person on the way. It's not much fun, but it sure beats having to do without any of those things during your holiday.

Sightseeing

The key to successful sightseeing is being realistic about how far you want to walk. Most people end up walking much farther on a city break than they would dream of doing in their own town or city. However, if you are exhausted by the end of day one, it will make day two much harder. It's not just about you, either – even if you can manage the walking, what about the other members of your party?

CASE STUDY: Overdoing it

When I was in Jerusalem, I did a walking tour of the Old City that took in a number of ancient sites and culminated at the Via Dolorosa, the path that Jesus followed to his crucifixion. I was particularly impressed by the pace set by an elderly lady, despite the intense July heat and the steep stairs and alleyways. However, when she reached the Church of the Holy Sepulchre, the site of Jesus' crucifixion, she collapsed in tears. The effort of the climb, combined with the emotion of the experience, had overwhelmed her.

Even though you may fancy yourself a traveller rather than a tourist, don't knock the city's open-topped bus tour, particularly if it's a 'hop on, hop off' one. They are the best way to see the main sights if you have limited time. Check the reviews on TripAdvisor to see how long the tour lasts and what the route is. If you are trying to fit some sightseeing into a business trip, or you don't speak the local language, these tours are your best bet. Even if you have more time to spend in the city, a bus tour can help you get your bearings, which will help you to do more exploring on foot later on.

I'd say it's also worth booking a tour for the particularly popular tourist sites, otherwise you're likely to spend several hours queuing to get in. On a tour you will usually be able to walk straight in with your guide and get lots of information from an expert who will point out details you probably wouldn't notice for yourself.

Even though you may feel you want to tick every box and see every last Greek vase in the Metropolitan Museum of Art, it's better to quit while you are ahead. Again, if you take this book's message to heart, most people will never see a fraction of what you will get to see over the course of your life and travels, so cut yourself some slack and leave some charge in your batteries for the rest of your trip.

Tourist information offices

As it happens, many open-top bus tours either leave from, or call in at, the local tourist information office. These are a godsend, particularly if you haven't been able to do much planning in advance. I think my wife and I must have called in on every single one in the country during our honeymoon in Scotland. Following their advice, we were able to stay in a huge range of places, from student halls of residence to grand hotels. They will usually give you good printed maps of the city centre that may be easier to follow than the map on your mobile, and they are useful for plotting a 'rocks and pebbles' route round the city (see an example in the Appendix).

What you also typically get from a tourist information office is insider knowledge of your destination, with tips on the more informal or lesser-known local events that may not have made it onto a website, plus intelligence on the best times to visit places, what might be closed for refurbishment and so on.

Capturing memories

Souvenirs

Lots of people will want to bring back some kind of trophy from their travels, and my family is no exception. Whatever you choose to buy – be it local crafts, kitsch souvenirs, pictures – I'd say go for things you know you will use or want to see every day. There's no point in hauling stuff back that's going to live in a drawer.

CASE STUDY: Tiny terrorist

In the UK there are a lot of kids' magazines that have toys attached to them. My wife absent-mindedly bought Jake one at the airport that had a gun stuck to it and put it in her bag. At customs the routine question 'Did you pack your own bags?' came up. Next thing we know, the woman operating the X-ray machine was declaring, 'He's got a gun in there!' The security man pulled out this plastic gun, and I tried to reassure him by saying we'd bought it at the airport... He just looked at me and said, 'Are you going to let him wave that around in the airport?' I said no, which was obviously the right answer, because he told us to put it back in the bag and be on our way.

For a long time we collected mugs, but when we could no longer fit any more into our cupboards, we switched to fridge magnets. Some of our highlights include one from the Surf Museum showing a VW van with a half-eaten surfboard on top, and a pirate ship from the Pirate Ship Dinner and Show. Our fridge is now double its original weight, but I wouldn't have it any other way.

Remember though that most souvenirs are not made in the location in which you are buying them, but more likely in a vast factory in a tax-exempt region of Greater Shanghai. This may not matter for some items, but you probably wouldn't want handicrafts that don't actually come from the area in which they are traditional.

T-shirts make great souvenirs. I wear my cool black Marine Corps Mud Run shirt a lot – it's a great conversation starter.

Photos

Landscapes can be beautiful, but I would always recommend taking photos with people in them. After years of printing out photos and putting them up around the house, I've noticed that I only ever print out those that show people I love, never those of just a view or a building. You are also far more likely to use the ones with people in them as a wallpaper, or to send them to a friend or family member to share as a memento of a trip.

I would also advise against spending too long lining up a shot. You can guarantee that the moment will pass – the bird will fly away, the child will make a face… With the camera on your phone, you can be as trigger-happy as you like, and there's a good chance that at least one of your shots will come out well. It's no use having photos that you don't look at. There are various online companies that can create printed photobooks from your photos, in formats ranging from small, sixteen-page softbacks, to albums with hard covers and hundreds of pages. These make great presents for people you've shared trips with.

Summary

Travel is much more fun if you've done your homework. You can't avoid nasty surprises and acts of God completely, but good preparation keeps these to a minimum and gives you the best chance of a trip that you can look back on fondly. To recap:

- Make sure you consult up-to-date timetables for every leg of your journey.
- The cheapest option may involve a longer journey, with more opportunities for disruptions and missed connections.
- Make sure you know when the shoulder season or low season dates are to get the best rates on bookings.
- Pace yourself (and the rest of your party) – you don't want to miss out on later stages of the trip by overdoing it at the beginning.
- Go for practical or genuinely appealing souvenirs, preferably locally made; you don't want to end up with things that just get stuffed in a drawer.
- Photos with people in them are better at capturing memories than empty landscapes, however beautiful.

Now you know how to go about planning for your leisure trip, and how to become a seasoned pro traveller. The world is at your fingertips; all you need to do now is decide where to go and what to do. Read on.

EIGHT
Take Your Pick

I was chatting with a work colleague a while back – as you might expect, asking him about what kind of a weekend he'd had. He said he and his family had been to the Mob Museum in Las Vegas. As it happened, we had already visited, but it seemed a bit rude to say, 'Been there, done that,' so instead I asked him what he had liked best about it. He answered, 'the Use of Force exhibit,' and described an interactive experience for two people in which you basically go from room to room, doing police training armed with a gun, dealing with the people who pop out of the screen at you. The last room was apparently the most amazing bit; you had to book it specifically and pay an extra $10, but he wouldn't tell me what happened in there – 'No spoilers,' he said.

Well, asking him about his visit certainly paid dividends. I immediately booked in for the Use of Force exhibit – and it turned out to be the most vivid memory of our trip because (spoiler alert) in the last room, there is a real flesh-and-blood person to deal with. You are warned that you could find it extremely stressful and reassured that you can withdraw if you want to. Laurie and I pressed on. We had a suspicious character on our hands in a so-called 'de-escalated situation', but our aim was to get him to put his hands in the air. I started talking to him, and he was mouthing off about his rights, not least his Second Amendment right to carry a gun – which we can see on his hip, and he's about to show us it. I'm told to draw my gun, then I realise that what he's holding is just a phone – in a room full of gun-toting urban terrorists! Super stressful. I was shaking for about half an hour afterwards.

Despite the extreme nature of this attraction, I'd still say to not knock it until you've tried it. Keeping an open mind about what attractions you might enjoy is the key to adding excitement to your plans.

A wide perspective

You never know what's going to capture your imagination and excitement. If you think of yourself as only interested in one type of activity or event, you could be missing out on an awful lot. Keep asking people questions all the time, even about things you've done before, as you never know what you may have missed or what you could do differently next time.

Don't forget, either, that your interests change as you go through life – something that fails to catch your interest now may well do so in the future. In terms of connecting with other people, finding out from them why they are passionate about an interest or activity that leaves you cold is always fun. Their insights and the strength of their commitment can sometimes change your mind.

Sports

I would describe my interests as running, cycling, socialising with friends and family, having adventures – and board games. When it comes to sport, I've tried most of them at least once, and I've been to see all manner of local professional teams in a variety of sports over the years, even some rather niche ones. These can have their own attraction for being less familiar – sumo wrestling is about as far from a fast-paced football game as it could be, but it's incredibly compelling. Often, it's not so much about the game being played, but about the people and atmosphere around you – just think of the English with cricket!

Personally, I like to have a balance between being a spectator of and participating in sports. I love watching arena football, but I also make sure that I map out the dates for public runs and cycle races that I'd like to take part in a year ahead.

Marvellous museums

What better demonstration of human ingenuity is there than our ability to create a museum devoted to just about anything?

There are a lot to choose from, but I'd say the maddest museums we've ever visited have to be:

- The Creation and Earth History Museum in Santee, CA (https://creationsd.org)
- The Museum of the Bible in Washington DC (www.museumofthebible.org)
- The Museum of Jurassic Technology in LA (http://mjt.org)
- The National World War I Museum in Kansas City (https://theworldwar.org)
- The Children's Museum of Phoenix, Arizona (https://childrensmuseumofphoenix.org/exhibits-and-experiences)
- Pinball Hall of Fame Museum in Las Vegas (https://pinballmuseum.org)
- Freemasons' Hall in London (www.ugle.org.uk/freemasons-hall)

TAKE YOUR PICK

- The Museum of Pop Culture in Seattle (www.mopop.org/)
- The National Videogame Museum in Dallas (https://nvmusa.org)

CASE STUDY: Dino drama

At the San Diego Zoo, there is a tar pit reconstruction that is interactive. On the walls around it are named three other museums in California that have collections related to this exhibit. Like many kids, my son Jake was enthralled with dinosaurs, so I organised a day trip to see all three of the museums mentioned in the exhibit. The last one, the Western Science Centre, was out in the desert at a remote reservoir. We were the only ones there, so we had a personal guided tour. We were invited into a domed room with no windows, where we sat in the centre on logs. Then all the lights went out – were we about to be sacrificed, I wondered?

Then the lights came up again in a glorious sunrise that completely surrounded us in the dome; it was like being inside an IMAX. A woolly mammoth came walking towards us, the sound was so loud that its footfalls resonated around my chest. That immersive display was a magical moment we'll never forget.

Museums are now light years away from the earlier dusty repositories of things in glass cases that you can look at but not touch. Most of the large ones have interactive displays and special exhibitions that allow you to get involved in a variety of practical and/or sensory ways. Even in the smaller ones you can now handle some of the exhibits – I think there's a special thrill that comes from touching an object that you know someone 500 years ago used in their everyday life.

Go with the flow

Although this book is all about planning activities and events to enrich your life, I don't want you to think you have to stick rigidly to these plans. Sometimes an unexpected opportunity turns up out of the blue, and you'd be mad not to follow it up. If you spot something interesting as part of your exploration of an area, you should listen to your instinct.

If you end up in the position of having to decide between attractions, remember the rock/pebble method. Is this new option a big, knockout rock that you simply have to see? Or is it a nice-to-have destination that you'll squeeze in somewhere if you can? If you can't make it somewhere on this occasion, make a note of it for the future.

TOP TIP

If you don't make a note of things that you've spotted that you'd like to see, you are bound to forget them, or only remember about them once the date for booking or for the event itself is past. My sure-fire method for not missing out on these attractions is to email myself a note about them at the moment; then I can transfer the date to my calendar later on, when I'm going through my emails. You always have access to your phone, and you will regularly check your emails so this works much better than filing a note away in a notepad or on an app.

Another reason for allowing some flexibility into your plans is in case you sense that someone in your group is not enjoying themselves. The goal is for everyone to have a fun time, so if you detect a lack of enthusiasm, it's best not to press on regardless. Instead, stop for refreshments, choose a shorter circuit or simply go home or back to wherever you're staying and chill.

Our weekend in Las Vegas was a great example of adapting to what was on offer and what we felt like doing, regardless of what I had planned. We'd just had a fantastic evening at the Ski Lodge, where the TV screens make it look as though snow is falling outside and everyone's wearing ski gear, and were heading back to the hotel for bed when I realised that we could go next door and take a look at the fabulous Aria hotel, so we did. While we were there, someone said, 'Do you want to go to the speakeasy at the Cosmopolitan?' 'Sure,' my wife said. Hang on – what happened to going home to bed?

We go in and of course the venue is great, because everything is wonderful at the Aria. There's a live guitarist on stage, playing classics from the eighties and nineties – and it's only Van Morrison! My wife, who is sitting all of ten yards from the stage, says, 'I hope he plays "Brown Eyed Girl",' and next thing you know Van Morrison says, 'I'll play "Brown Eyed Girl" for you in a minute...' My itinerary had ended at the Ski Lodge, but how much we'd have missed out on if we hadn't followed our instincts – we had a wonderful night.

CASE STUDY: In praise of the Pantheon

While I was on a five-day break in Rome, I took every opportunity I could to visit the Pantheon, a well-preserved Roman temple that has served as a Catholic church since 609 CE. I've always been fascinated by the building, and as Rome's city centre is so compact, I could pop back into it whenever I happened to be visiting a site nearby.

On my second-to-last day in Rome, I had been visiting the Villa Farnesina to see Raphael's stunning fresco 'The Triumph of Galatea' when a massive thunderstorm broke out. We (my then girlfriend and I) ran all the way back to the Pantheon, getting soaked, but it was worth it to see the lightning illuminating the inside of the vast concrete dome and the rain pouring through the oculus (the hole in the roof) and then running off into little brass drains set into the floor that I'd never noticed before – a fabulous experience.

Knowing when to give in to others' wishes, and when it would do no harm to stand your ground, is an art. You will get better at it the more you do it. The whole point of my approach, though, is that your adventures should be organised but not regimented. Leave some room for manoeuvre, for yourself and others.

Curiosity

As children we are endlessly curious. 'How does this work?' 'What happens if I press that button?' Sadly, this quality can desert us as we get older and the responsibilities come crowding in. Yet if you're not curious, you will miss so much of what's going on around you, so it's worth exercising that rusty curiosity muscle to get it working again. We talk of 'idle curiosity', which makes it sound trivial, but curiosity provides so many opportunities for learning. The next time you wonder fleetingly about some process, place or person, follow it up. Google and other search engines make this possible in a way we would never have dreamed of a few decades ago.

Encourage children's curiosity, too. If you notice that they are interested in a topic, see if you can incorporate it into a visit or an outing. It's remarkable how often someone will attribute their success in their field, or the lifelong passion that is a source of joy and contentment to them, to having their interest sparked as a child.

CASE STUDY: Music and more

> It was when my son was studying the violin that I discovered the existence of the Museum of Making

Music. As part of a corporate building on an industrial estate in Carlsbad, California, it didn't look promising from the outside, but it was fantastic when we got inside. Far from detailing the history of the violin and the piano, it's mostly about the instruments of big marching bands. It documents how, in the days before radio, every town in the USA had several marching bands, and band instruments were sold in their millions. Every child played an instrument back in the mid-1800s, practising during the week and playing in parks, fully decked out in uniform, at the weekend. It was a glimpse into a lost world, and well worth a visit.

Curiosity is also a good way of recognising and resisting the extent to which the information we receive through our devices is dictated by algorithms. Those cunning devils totally failed to predict that, following the fun of my foray into medieval archery, I could be tempted to take an interest in blacksmithing! (I am now the proud owner of a hand-forged bottle opener – forged, in fact, by my own fair hand!)

Hobbies and projects

Although this book has focused on planning for leisure activities and recreational travel, it would be wrong to ignore what the more everyday hobbies and projects have to offer as constructive and enjoyable ways of making good use of your time. There are significant differences between the two, though.

Hobbies

One research study identified that most hobbies only last sixteen months,[13] and it's true that people do tend to go through a lot of hobbies. The lucky ones are those that find an enduring interest that will last them a lifetime. The benefits of hobbies are wide-ranging; they offer opportunities for:

- Socialising (sports, choirs, amateur dramatics)
- Solitude (fishing, hiking, DIY)
- Skill development
- Greater involvement in your community
- Personal satisfaction from focusing temporarily on your own needs
- Relaxation

The open-endedness of hobbies can be a key part of their attraction. You don't need to let the fact that you're not very good at something get in the way of your enjoyment. No one should be measuring you or passing judgement.

---

13 J Mitchell, 'All the gear, no idea! Britain's hobbies have a shelf life of 16 months' (British Heart Foundation, 15 January 2019), www.bhf.org.uk/what-we-do/news-from-the-bhf/news-archive/2019/january/britains-hobbies-have-a-shelf-life-of-16-months, accessed January 2025

Beware of sticking with a hobby when it's no longer giving you satisfaction. If you have been pursuing a hobby for a while, particularly one with high setup costs (photography or sailing, for example, as opposed to yoga), it can be hard to walk away. However, if you're no longer enjoying it, give yourself permission to give it up. It's far better to move on from it emotionally than to find yourself resenting something you once loved. The time and money you have invested are behind you; what matters is the future.

Projects

While hobbies have no overall goal, projects always have an end in mind. Projects involve moving a ball forwards, be that for yourself, your family or work. They can be mundane (but nevertheless important), such as my project to consolidate all the little pension pots I have into one, so that I can see what is going on and know what financial planning I need to do, or they can be exciting, like planning a family weekend away.

CASE STUDY: Not just a door

You wouldn't think replacing a door in our front room would be a project, but it certainly turned into one. Because the door in question was not a standard size, I first reached out to four different custom door companies, but couldn't get a quote out of any of them. Eventually, I found a house for sale in the community that I live in and discovered, when I went to the open house, that it had exactly the door that I wanted. I emailed the realtor, who then asked the owner of the house where they had got their door from (remember, just ask!). It took me several attempts, and I had to keep putting notes in my calendar reminding me to reach out to him to keep the whole enterprise on the boil. In the end, it took four months for the custom door to be made, in Colorado, then I had to have a fitter come out, then a second carpenter to finish it and, finally, it was painted. This is how an apparently trivial household task became a major project!

The bonus of treating tasks like replacing my door as projects is that an organised approach always yields a better result than a haphazard one and so, especially with home improvements, it's far less likely to lead to an outcome you might regret.

Just as you would at work, the key to managing a project successfully is breaking it down into the steps you need to take and working out a timeline for each, recognising the order they need to be done in. I find that my planner is a great help with this, as I can save all the notes for a project in one place and populate my calendar with the milestone dates.

How many projects you have on the go at one time will depend on your circumstances, and you may feel you don't have time for any personal projects at all. However, I still feel it's good to be working towards a goal, and it's motivating to have something to look forward to.

Summary

The wider you cast your net, the more likely you are to find activities that can be a source of enjoyment for years to come.

- Keep an open mind and don't assume that some kinds of activity are not for you; you might be surprised at what you enjoy.

- Ask people about the things that they've enjoyed; they may give you insights that you couldn't get elsewhere.

- Don't overlook museums. There is such a range of them now, all with their own highly creative attractions – you're sure to find one to your taste.

- Be spontaneous and embrace unexpected opportunities. You wouldn't want to miss out on something exciting for the sake of sticking rigidly to your plans.

- Develop your curiosity – it could lead you in all sorts of interesting directions.

- Hobbies and projects are different, but they both have the potential to enrich your life in various ways.

The aim of the advice in this chapter is to increase your overall happiness and wellbeing, and those of your family, of course. In the next chapter, we'll be exploring the nature of happiness, and how personal planning for your leisure time contributes to this.

NINE
Happiness

While I was writing this book, we decided to decorate our downstairs corridor. We did all the painting ourselves and it took nine months. We have a rule in the Unthank family: don't do it yourself if someone else can do it better, especially DIY. For some reason, I forgot to apply the rule to this project and learned something important: I may be good at accounting, but I'm certainly not good at decorating.

As part of the redecoration, my wife wanted to cover the bare walls with a collage of family photos and bought eighty small picture frames. She then tasked me with finding photos from our past to fill them. After twenty years of marriage (and like most people, we have thousands of digital photos) it was a huge undertaking to sift through and decide what to include.

I dreaded this task and kept procrastinating, finding a million other things to do, but eventually I couldn't put it off any longer. I sat down to put photos on a shortlist and, as I started going through them, I was struck and overwhelmed by all the fun times we have had together. The photos were full of wonderful sites, hikes, museums and more, but it was recalling the memories of what had taken place at each of those locations that flooded me with so much happiness.

One photo was taken in the basement restaurant of the Sacramento State Capitol. I'd asked my wife if she wanted a drink. She'd said no but she kept reaching for and drinking mine. When she looked away I deliberately moved it just out of her reach; she instinctively reached for it, realised it had moved and we caught each other's eye and burst into laughter.

Then there was the picture of my son on the balcony at the top of the New Orleans WW2 museum, way up above the planes and tanks. I remembered how my nine-year-old had looked out over the parapet, seen how far away the floor below us was and said 'Dad, Dad, my bum keeps going up and down, up and down.' Mine was too – it was a long way down! We quickly left for the safety of the ground floor.

Going back further, there was my son at age six, watching a medieval gladiator fight, holding my hand over his face because he could not take the suspense, but still peeking between my fingers.

I also loved the pictures of our homemade volcano science project, exploding uncontrollably and spraying 'lava' all over the kitchen, while my wife shielded the baby, giggling the whole time.

And not forgetting all the photos of family and friends from my trips back to the UK…

I noticed that all the photos I most cherished were of people, of memories shared and good times with those I loved most. All these memories and all these good times are what make me happy.

Happiness as a goal

Happiness is the whole point of my approach to personal planning. With all the events captured in the photos, I had looked forward to them during the planning process, enjoyed the activities and reunions while they were happening and now I was recalling them with immense pleasure.

As happiness is the ultimate goal of enriching your life in this way, it's worth exploring how we experience happiness, and what your own approach to it might be. The Ancient Greeks knew a thing or two about happiness; their word *eudaimonia* translates literally as 'a state of good spirit' and, according to the philosopher Aristotle, this inferred the highest possible human good.

What can you do if you realise that your resting level of happiness is not that high? I would return here to my father's saying, which I quoted at the beginning of the book: 'Anyone can be... miserable. It takes no effort at all.' To distance yourself from what is causing you dissatisfaction or unhappiness you need to act, to move. Start by setting up something to look forward to – perhaps re-establishing contact with a friend, because nothing is better for your health and wellbeing than connectedness.

The friction of life

It's unreasonable to think that you can be happy all of the time; we can all expect our fair share of distressing events and negative circumstances in our lives. To mitigate the impact of these when they arise, it helps to have close friends and family to help you through – and in turn, you should be prepared to offer them that same support. These bonds are mutually reinforcing.

Even in circumstances such as a life-changing illness or accident, people tend to adapt and make the best of their circumstances. How often do we hear of people who have been physically impaired in an accident, say, embracing the opportunity to get involved in sports for people with disabilities, or in awareness campaigns? Yet it's just as easy to identify people who apparently have little cause for dissatisfaction with their lives yet are nevertheless not particularly happy most of the time.

CASE STUDY: Recovery period

The wife of a friend of mine had a mental health crisis that fundamentally altered her personality, turning her into someone different from the woman he'd married. Their lives were diverging and, after a while, she left him.

He was devastated. He was crying all the time, and claimed he could not conceive of a world in which he could live without her. However, over time, his distress receded and he is now happier than at any time since I've known him. He no longer has to cope with the uncertainty of his wife's moods and is able to plan for the things that make him happy. Hardly a week goes by without him telling me that he has signed up for a fun run or some such activity. The saying, 'Time heals all wounds' may be a cliché, but it's true if you allow it to be.

When tragedy strikes, try to look for the little things that will get you back on an even keel. Go for a hike in the nearest countryside, bake yourself a cake… and if you don't have any ideas, ask other people. You'll get both useful suggestions, and an added point of connection with that person, so it's well worth doing.

There's an analogy that describes this process perfectly, and it's the concept of 'kedging'. Imagine that you are sailing a boat and it runs aground on the sand. What you need to do in that situation is throw out an anchor so that it lodges in the sand in deeper water; then you can use the rope or chain to pull your boat afloat again. If you're in the doldrums, think of some small adventure or treat that you can use to drag yourself out of it and back to a happier place. I'd recommend something manageable, achievable and local.

Positively charged

I'm sure you're all familiar with concepts like the power of positive thinking, reframing your thoughts and improving your mindset. I'm a big fan of these ideas, though I find that some of the claims about manifesting and so on tend towards the fantastical, or at least more akin to wishful thinking.

Books like Napoleon Hill's *Think and Grow Rich* make it all sound easy,[14] but I do believe that if you want something enough, you tell other people about it often, you write it down to ensure you remember how much you want it and you break down the steps required to achieve it into tasks that you then include

---

14   N Hill, *Think and Grow Rich* (Capstone, 2010)

on your planning list, it will most likely come to pass. Some years ago, I came across somebody who certainly wasn't letting themselves forget exactly what they wanted: they had printed out on a piece of paper the words 'I will make $100,000 this year' and stuck it on the steering wheel of their car. That was what they were confronted with every time they got in the car to go to work, or on a leisure trip.

I think there's a much more down-to-earth explanation for the success of these techniques than some of their prophets like to admit. Keeping your goals front and centre in your mind means that you are always on the lookout for connections to what you want to do, and will therefore be well placed to take advantage of things when they come up. If you're telling other people about your goals, they will think of you if an opportunity arises (though don't be obnoxious about it and badger them). My Israel trip that I mentioned earlier is proof that this works.

Have grit...

You'll run up against obstacles to your plans all the time, and how you react to them depends to a large extent on personality. For some people, barriers act like a red rag to a bull and they become more determined than ever to get their own way. Others just roll over and give up. I think that makes you a bit of a marshmallow, and in the end, it won't make you happy. There is something uniquely rewarding about prevailing against all the odds.

But though it's sometimes important to show some grit and stick with things to get the ultimate reward and satisfaction of, say, completing a physical challenge you've set yourself, there is no joy to be found in gritting your teeth and persevering with something that your heart is no longer in.

.... but don't grin and bear it

Bearing in mind the sunk cost fallacy (when someone is reluctant to abandon a project or an activity because of all the time and/or money they've already invested in it, even when it's obvious that doing so would be the better option), you need to be clear in your mind about the nature of the obstacles you are facing. Are they genuine problems like lack of availability, other people's fluctuating calendars and acts of God like inclement weather? Or is it simply that the quantity of paperwork needed, for example, is making you feel a bit fainthearted? If it's the latter, then you need to decide how much you want it and either power on through the challenge, or recognise that deep down you don't think it's worth it and cut your losses.

CASE STUDY: On your bike

My friend Bobby lived for cycling, and for more than a decade he did little else. Then he suddenly fell out of love with it, but walking away wasn't easy: his whole identity had been bound up with cycling. My advice to him was, 'If you're looking at your bike and it's making you miserable, just stop doing it and start doing whatever it is you want to do instead. It's not as though you're doing it for anyone else, so what are you waiting for?'

You're only on this planet for so long, and you need to give yourself permission to give up on things and try something different. If ever I were to write an actual business book, I would call it *Fail Fast*, because I've learned that it's far more effective to acknowledge straight away that something isn't working out than to keep flogging a dead horse. Pride should play no part in your decision-making when it comes to pursuing happiness. Edison's widely quoted proud boast is a great example of a positive perspective on failing: 'I have not failed. I've just found 10,000 ways that won't work.'[15]

Don't beat yourself up

One of the biggest threats to our happiness and well-being is our tendency to brood over things. Something happens, or someone says something, and a persistent regret or sense of guilt gets lodged in our heads, colouring our thinking and possibly inhibiting our

---

15 Recounted in FL Dyer and TC Martin, *Edison: His Life and Inventions* (1910)

actions. Yet most of the time we have blown it up out of all proportion, and whatever the incident was will have barely registered with anyone else.

Many years ago my brother was having a bit of a hard time and he'd taken it out on me, basically being pretty horrible to me, until I'd had enough. The next time he appeared at my door, I said: 'Like I have any interest in anything you have to say.' He went away.

I discovered later that he'd wanted to tell me that he was about to become a father. He'd come to give me some fantastic news, and I'd just been rude and sent him on his way. I carried the guilt about the way I'd behaved for fifteen years, but when I eventually expressed my remorse to him at his stag do, he couldn't even remember that this had happened.

Perhaps another moral of this story is that if you feel you have wronged or slighted someone in any way, apologise as soon as you realise you have done it. This will nip your sense of guilt in the bud so that you don't needlessly torture yourself as I did, as well as, once again, enhancing your connection with another person.

Keep moving

To be able to fully enjoy the widest possible range of activities, it's important to keep as fit as you can.

Sitting behind a desk all day is not the best way to keep mobile, but it's what many of us have come to accept. Especially now, post-Covid, many of us often don't even need to travel anywhere to work. As a result, getting enough exercise – of the right kind – takes conscious effort, but it's worth it.

TOP TIP

If you've got a car, you maintain it, put the right fuel in it and have it serviced. Your body is your vehicle for moving around in this world, and if it's rusting, you'll have fewer adventures and less ability to do things.

Top of my list of recommended reading on this subject is a book called *Younger Next Year: Live strong, fit, sexy, and smart – until you're 80 and beyond*.[16] The theory behind it is that if you don't get out of that chair, you won't get out of that chair. By following the programme, you can learn how to defer most of the problems of ageing, such as weakness, sore joints and poor balance, as well as avoid much serious disease and illness, all through – no prizes for guessing – diet, exercise and building (and maintaining) emotional connections.

Despite our best efforts, disease can creep up on us. This is why I've signed up for a regular full body

---

16   AJ Hamilton MD, C Crowley and HS Lodge, *Younger Next Year: Live strong, fit, sexy, and smart – until you're 80 and beyond*, 2nd revised edition (Workman Adult, 2019)

health check: there are too many diseases out there that do not give you any symptoms until it's too late – a problem which is made worse by men's tendency to suffer in silence. That's not the way to a long and happy life. However, should the worst happen, adapt and look for workarounds. It's better to get out and walk with a stick, if you can, than to sit at home and feel sorry for yourself.

Last, but not least, I can't improve on Anne Frank's words about happiness: 'Whoever is happy will make others happy.'[17] It's not selfish to attend to your own happiness – others will thank you for it.

Summary

It turns out there are many things you can do to promote your own happiness and that of those around you.

- Having something to look forward to is the best way to avoid feelings of boredom or despondence.
- Positive thinking is not magic, but it is useful to keep your mind on your goals.
- Building emotional connections is vitally important for happiness and wellbeing.

---

17 A Frank, *The Diary of a Young Girl* (Penguin Classics, 2019)

- Don't agonise about things. Most of the stuff you regret or feel guilty about has probably been completely forgotten by everybody else.
- Keep fit so that you can get out and about to enjoy all the world has to offer. If need be, adapt to your circumstances by taking advantage of workarounds and technology now available for people with physical limitations.

Conclusion

After completing this book, you now have no excuse not to get out there and do stuff. Looking back over these chapters has felt a bit like drowning – I have seen my life flashing before my eyes, but in the best possible way.

Looking back, I realise how much I've changed since making the decision to be more proactive in what I did with my free time. Whereas previously I felt I was drifting and that life was a great big party going on somewhere else that I wasn't invited to, now I feel fully in control. From that first tentative list of five goals for the following year I've gone from strength to strength, growing in confidence and ambition as my plans have come to fruition.

The benefits of my proactive personal planning have spilled over into all areas of my life. That greater sense of direction encouraged me to take bolder steps in my career – and to take the plunge when I recognised that I had met 'The One'. Without a doubt, it's this approach to life that has allowed me to achieve everything I have so far.

I've had more than my fair share of excitement and adventure over the last decades – some of which has called on reserves of stoicism and fortitude I never knew I had – but it would be hard to overstate how rewarding the increased connectedness that has come along with this has been. I've managed to maintain my friendships with people from my student years and my early days in the workplace – this is rare, particularly for men, even in the current era of social media. Even the shared hardships of adventures that don't quite go to plan are great at creating and cementing strong friendships. I've built new relationships and become an involved member of the communities I live and work in. Interestingly, the doctor who carried out my health check told me that the four factors vital for longevity are genetics, blood pressure control, daily exercise and having a connected life, so there's a clear scientific endorsement of my approach.

Finally, although I now live on the other side of the world from my extended family, I am as close to them as ever. In mid-life, it's easy to get overwhelmed by your commitments and let various things go. My philosophy is to keep thinking about your nearest and dearest, keep talking to them and keep looking for opportunities to include them in your activities.

Though it may be hard to detect in a teenager, I feel sure that my zest for life has rubbed off on my son. Right from the start he has been exposed to the notion that you go out and make your own opportunities. All the scout badges he has done have given him a solid idea of where his interests lie, and it certainly helps to be going out into the world with experience of other countries, other communities and other points of view. The sense of continuity that runs from my dad's 'It doesn't take any effort at all to be miserable' to the positive habits that my son will be able to carry into his adulthood fills me with joy.

I'm sure, too, that he has observed the power of simply asking for what you want (politely, of course) as opposed to being reticent and simply hoping that what you want will somehow fall into your lap. He's also seen that it's not the end of the world when things go wrong – it wouldn't be a proper Unthank family holiday without at least one disaster!

My curiosity has fed on itself: discovering new things has led to more things to be curious about, and gradually the gaps in my understanding of how the world works, how systems interact, how people tick, are being filled in. I'll never get to the bottom of it all, but that doesn't matter, because the quest itself is so rewarding.

I have plenty more adventures planned for the future – my list for next year seems to have doubled in just a matter of weeks. Just this weekend, Laurie and I managed to sit down together, set our holiday dates in stone and agree on all the things we want to do, including hiring an RV, jet skiing to Catalina Island, catching up with friends and more. There's just so much to look forward to, whether it's high-octane sports or simply browsing around a new bookshop in the neighbourhood.

Now it's over to you. What I want for you is to have that sense that the world is your oyster, and that all you have to do is go out and taste it. If you stay locked into an autopilot existence of work/sleep/repeat, you'll miss out on the party that your life could be. If I've helped persuade just one person of all the possibilities that are out there, this book project will have been well worth it. So what are you waiting for? Get a pen and paper, or grab your phone, and start making a list of all those things you've always wanted to do. Good luck… and have fun!

Appendix 1 – Two-Day Tour Of New York

I plotted a route around New York using Stephen Covey's rocks and pebbles concept to prioritise the attractions, so as to be sure of fitting in as many of them as possible. I have provided this below for you as an example of how you can stack rocks and pebbles to get the most out of your trip days.

Itinerary for day one

Starting point: 215 Pearl St, NY (this is where we were staying)

- Wall Street – rock
- Bull statue – pebble
- 9/11 Memorial – rock

GET A LIFE

- One World Trade Center (decided not to visit the observation deck) – pebble
- Subway to Central Park
- Tour of Central Park – pebble
- Hotdog in the park – pebble
- The Metropolitan Museum of Art (Met) – rock
- Lunch at the Met – pebble
- Guggenheim – pebble (an unforeseen opportunity that time allowed)
- Natural History Museum – rock
- Subway home

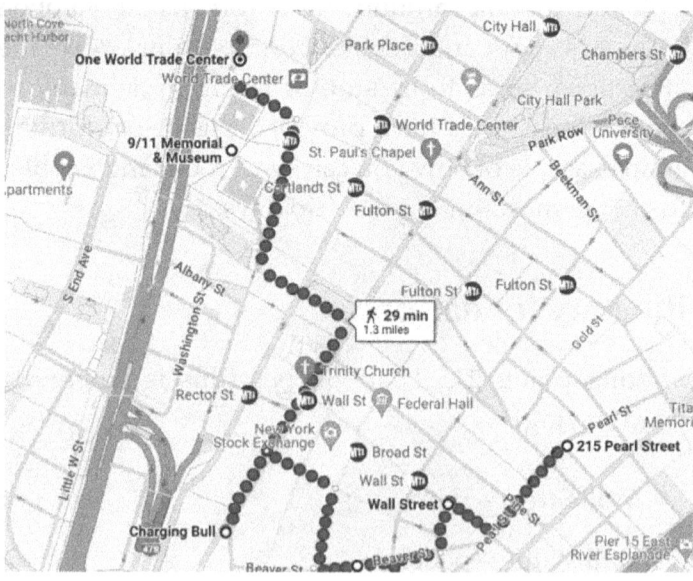

251 Pearl Street to World Trade Center site

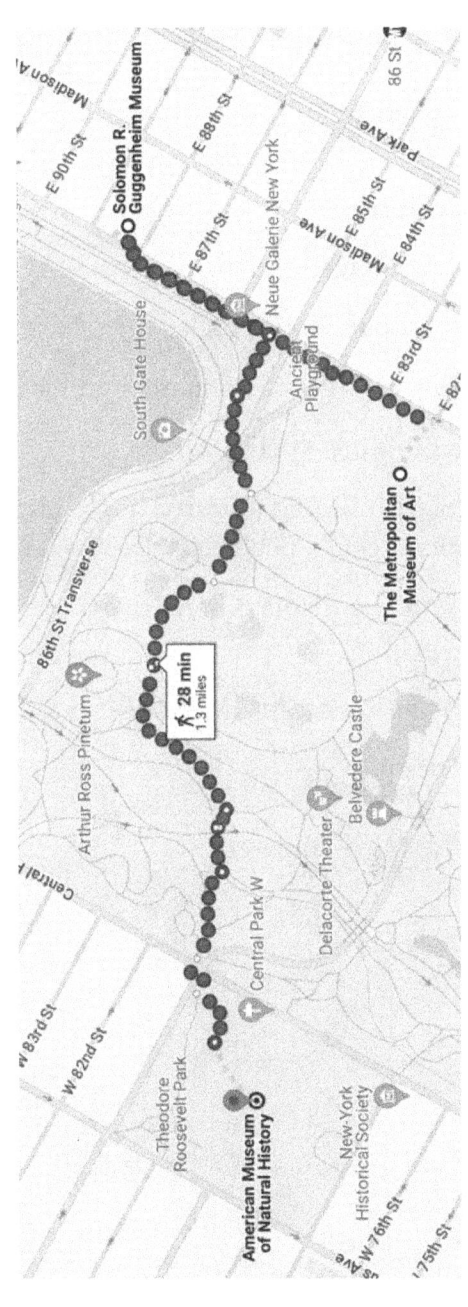

Guggenheim Museum to Natural History Museum

GET A LIFE

Itinerary for day two

Starting point: 215 Pearl St

- Katz's Delicatessen – rock
- Greenwich Village – pebble
- The Strand Book Store – rock
- Chess Hustlers in Union Square – pebble
- Flat Iron Building – pebble
- Empire State Building (decided not to hit the observation deck) – pebble
- Macy's Window displays and Time Square – pebble
- Museum of Modern Art (MoMA) – rock
- Subway home

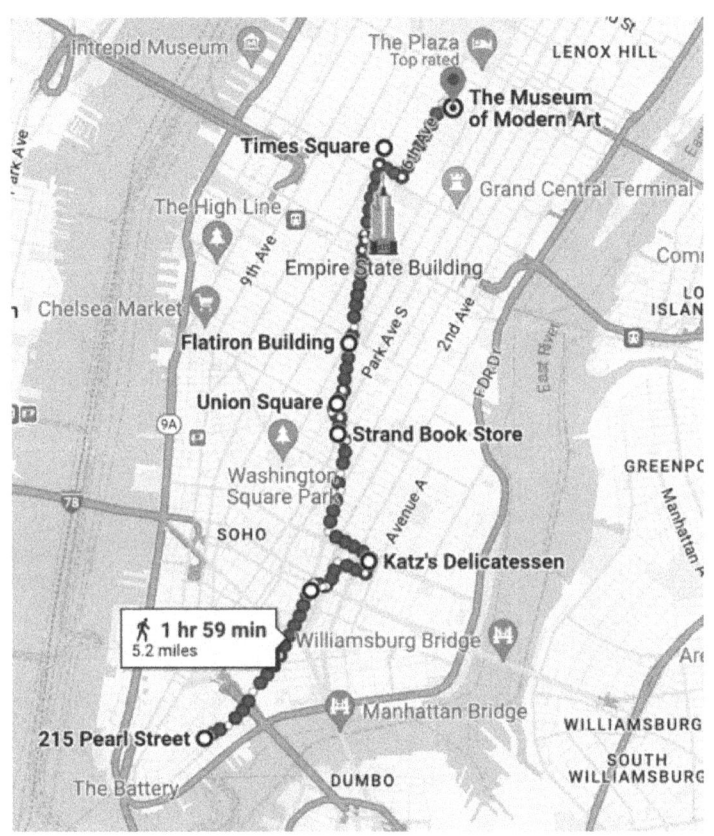

215 Pearl Street to the Museum of Modern Art

Appendix 2 – Checklists

Travelling abroad

You are not likely to forget passports and money, but some overseas travel requirements, such as inoculations, entail a bit of planning and lead time. For example:

- Passports
- Photo(copy) of your passports
- Visas
- Currency and cards (a credit card rather than a debit card for car hire)
- Driving licence

- Inoculations (and evidence of)
- Plugs, adapters and cables
- Phone
- Insurance
- Medication

Travelling with children

Travel for children is tough on them and tough on you. You may need to relax your rules about screen time, snacks and so on. The following items need to be in your hand luggage on a flight, or easily accessible on any other form of transport.

- Wet wipes/facecloth
- Toys
- Attachment object (for example, teddy, blanket)
- Comics and activity books
- Change(s) of clothes
- Plastic bags/nappy sacks
- Snacks/baby formula

Camping and hiking

- Appropriate shoes/boots
- Crocs/sneakers
- Clothing layers, including warm/waterproof clothing
- Socks – more pairs than you think you need
- Mosquito netting
- Insect repellent
- Water purifying tablets
- First aid kit, including plasters and antichafing stick
- Power pack for your phone
- Compass
- Paper maps
- Water bottle

Resources

Printed materials

- Dorling Kindersley Top Ten Guides: My go-to guide for a new city, especially overseas, as they highlight the most important sites, alongside food and culture highlights. Good for research when you're planning a trip, and when you're finalising your itinerary.
- Locally produced maps and brochures from tourist information offices; these often contain details not available elsewhere.
- National Geographic guides are great for trips to National Parks.

- Second-hand copies of Rough Guides, Michelin guides and Rick Steves' guides can be found on eBay – though note that some information could be dated.

- USGS topographical maps.

Digital

- Amtrak: Timetables and fares for railways across the US.

- Expedia: Price comparison for flights and packages including flights, car hire and accommodation.

- Google Flights.

- Google searches of blogs on city itineraries – invaluable for finding other people's discoveries.

- The Man in Seat 61: Although based in Europe, this website can also help with planning beyond Europe.

- Tourist information offices for your destination.

- TripAdvisor: Practical information is supplemented with personal insights and responses regarding accommodation, restaurants and attractions.

Planners

- Large month-view wall calendar – this is ideal for displaying family and school timings in a shared area.

- Leuchtturm: Good-quality planners and notebooks.

- Moleskine: My go-to is the XL monthly planner, with two pages per month and two pages for notes between months. It also has about sixty blank pages after the monthly view for all your notes.

- Rhodia: Planners with premium-quality paper for people who use heavy-ink pens.

Acknowledgements

Thank you for finding this book and reading it. Writing *Get A Life* has been an adventure in and of itself.

Most importantly, I want to thank my wife, Laurie, the love of my life, who has always supported me and my desire to experience new cities, new activities and new museums. She never gets bored, is incredibly patient and always immense fun to be around.

I'm eternally grateful to the scouting movement, through whom my Eagle Scout son Jake and I have explored America's great outback, met even greater lifelong friends and spent quality 'father and son' time together. Watching Jake mature into a young man through scouting has been one of the greatest privileges of my life.

I'd like to thank my parents for always being so supportive and for teaching me not to dwell on my problems but to solve them myself: my dad, who was the smartest person I ever met and also the most patient, and my mum, whose no-nonsense view of the world always puts problems in perspective (and whose cooking is world class).

I'd also like to thank my brothers, Richard, Tony and Julian, for being there for me, always being on my side and never saying 'I told you so.'

I am fortunate to still have my best friend from college in my life. Andy Harwin was the inspiration for my first personal list, even if, all these years later, he can't remember suggesting it. He should take all the credit. Andy has been there through the good times and the bad, and I will always be thankful for his friendship.

Thanks, too, to all the friends that I have dragged along on my adventures: those who are still in my life, like Dave Corbett, Dave Beamish, James Wood, Dalen Meeter, Tony Moldanado and Andre Bruckner; and those who were part of my life for years but fell away as lives and locations diverged – Graham, Gwendal and Matt, I wish you all the best.

Family is everything, and I include my close friends in that description. Thank you all, and I hope for many more adventures to come.

The Author

A dual US and UK national, Phillip is a chief financial officer with diverse business experience on both sides of the Atlantic. Originally from the UK, he grew up as part of a large army family that instilled into him a sense of discipline, integrity and adaptability.

Now living in sunny San Diego, Phillip has a passion for ongoing education and his dedication to self-development has seen him add an impressive array of qualifications to his original degree in Ocean Science with Astronomy, including a law degree, certification as a Chartered Accountant in both the US and the UK, and certification as a treasurer.

In his twenties, Phillip discovered a love for travel and adventure that has remained an important part of his life – alongside a love for an American, Laurie, who is *the* most important part of his life. He moved to America to marry Laurie and together they have a teenage son, Jake, and a golden retriever, James.

Continually juggling a demanding career with family life, Phillip is always looking for ways to make the most of his limited vacation time, ensuring that every moment is filled with meaningful experiences.

His journey, and this book, reflect a commitment to continuous learning and personal growth – a journey of knowledge and experiences that he wants to share with you, the reader. Whether he's exploring new destinations or enhancing his professional skills, Phillip's story is one of dedication, curiosity and a zest for life.

in www.linkedin.com/in/phillipunthank

www.ingramcontent.com/pod-product-compliance
Lightning Source LLC
Chambersburg PA
CBHW050111170426
43198CB00014B/2531